Personal Journey

Personal Jouney
Doug Rucker
Layout by Helane Freeman

Copyright © 2016 Doug Rucker
All rights reserved.

Doug Rucker
Vilimapubco
Malibu, CA
ruckerdoug@gmail.com

For permission requests, sales to U.S. bookstores and wholesalers,
or to inquire about quantity discounts, please contact the publisher
at the email address above.

Printed in the United States of America

Library of Congress Control Number: 2016915719

ISBN 978-0-9968060-4-6

First Edition
10 9 8 7 6 5 4 3 2 1

Personal Journey

Doug Rucker

To Seekers of the Soul

Contents

PART 3 - RUMINATIONS

PART 4 - DILEMMA

PART 5 - RISKING

PART 8 - ACCEPTANCE

Personal Journey

Introduction

*T*his book is about the most challenging task we human beings face – finding and becoming one with our own true selves. Clinical evidence indicates that this most elusive part of ourselves is strongly influenced by those around us. It is clear that our earliest relationships, when we are least able to control and consciously respond to what is happening, are frequently the most influential. From infancy on, as we respond and are responded to, we learn to conform in order to be accepted by our caregivers and survive. Frequently, what we conclude is that there are things about ourselves which are unacceptable and must be kept secret. Ironically, these repressed aspects of ourselves may be the very dualities we need most to be effective adults living full and satisfying lives. If our lives become too uncomfortable, we may even embark on a search to reconnect with our secret and deeply hidden true selves. This search is the *Personal Journey* described in this book.

As the author notes in Precursors, he started writing poems on a *'what the hell'* whim, and seemed unaware that, even in his very first poem, *A Clear Picture*, his inner purpose was already established; to search for the *'real self,'* his *'IT.'* Being of a philosophic turn of mind, his poems questioned the meaning of life in general and the joys and struggles of his own life in particular. Still, he seemed not to recognize a growing awareness of an inner self becoming ever more insistent and finally appearing full face in *Dream, Discovery, Insight*.

In his life, personal changes began to happen almost without conscious awareness, causing conflict and confusion.

The author felt an ever-growing urge to reach out for new relationships, and reach deep within for inner truths. The poems in *Ruminations* and *Dilemma* express this struggle, and confront him with his unexamined inner being in *The Heartsore*.

In *Risking* and *Discovery* he enters the darker chambers of his deeper mind. His poems become more obscure. He finds himself adopting an *'automatic writing'* style in the manner of Theodore Roethke, and then discovers that he can decipher these seemingly unconnected poetic lines through a method of interpretation which connects with his dreams. These lead directly to his deepest core. The mysteries of his own psychological dynamic are revealed, freeing him to love.

In *Processing* and *Acceptance*, the poems express his climb toward integration and wholeness. The poetic style becomes more direct - humorous, philosophic, imaginative - leaving us, finally, with the powerful image of *The Jumper*, a man of consummate self-confidence, uniqueness and courage.

In sharing such a journey, and the poetry which was his vehicle of passage, the author offers the reader an opportunity to glimpse one man's effort to find himself. This book illustrates an expressive and creative method, which those so inclined may adapt to their own use as they embark on their own *Personal Journey*.

Marge Lewi-Rucker, M. A., ATR, MFCC

Foreword

I wish to share with you the poems, feelings, thoughts and discoveries I made during a period of intense personal growth in the four years between 1976 and 1980. I was 48 years old in 1976, a Malibu architect doing residential work. I was married and had three daughters, ages 12, 14 and 16.

Ten years earlier, in 1966, my new doctor took me off tranquilizers I'd been taking for hypertension under another doctor's orders, and I sustained an explosion of new experiences. I made a creative departure from my usual architectural work and designed a *'pedestal'* house for my family overlooking Surfrider Beach, took up surfboarding, joined a chorus singing renaissance music, began making water colors and, what-the-hell, writing poetry. I called it *'making poetic-ness,'* and still do. My close friend, Rick Davidson, was risking writing poetry, and to be a good poet I can't be afraid to write a bad poem, right? What had I to lose? I'd try it.

The first poem I ever wrote is the first one in this book. Webster defines a poem as *a composition in verse; lofty or imaginative writing or artistic expression.* I'm not sure any of the works in this book qualify under that definition. I did enjoy writing them and ultimately they served to help me solve some very troubling personal problems. They were not only an outlet for strong feelings, but led to a method of uncovering *rules* learned early in childhood which were not only not applicable any more, but growth-inhibiting and detrimental to understanding of self. For this reason alone, they are worth my time.

This book should be considered a sharing of a personal experience. It is my intent to open a window into my brain and soul through which you may briefly look; to satisfy whatever curiosity you may have, to spark your personal thoughts and perhaps to elicit whatever dialogue we may subsequently have, which I would enjoy.

Part 1 - Precursors

A CLEAR PICTURE

Your attitude determines
the cleanliness of the window
through which you see the light of day.

For a cleaner window
you must first know
the window is dirty.

You may discover the window is dirty if
      past fortune allows you to sense it,
      or
      you are convinced by outer forces,
agents of the brighter light,
      that it is.

You will clean that window to the degree
      you are dissatisfied.

Study the relativity of all things.
A little each day will do the job.

And yet, I can't do it.
The pain is insufficient.
I haven't the slenderest curiosity.
My window is shady at best,
      or dark,
      or encrusted,
      or all three.

Must I, too, wait for agents?
Shall I recognize them?

Vainly hope, perhaps, for some
  latent curiosity to save me?

Perhaps my window ever dirtier
will cause the pain to make me clean.
Shall I then only scrub
  'til pain is bearable again?

And what if my real self,
  my *"IT,"*
  is more satisfied,
  unsatisfied?

  Can I undo that too?

Perhaps we are as Buddhists say,
  the River,
  deep and shallow,
  cool and warm.

AGE OF ANXIETY

10/66

I get up early.
The hostile sun
declares the day's vitality.

My being rises to my throat
and spreads to the extremities
filling every void with juice.
My eyes with tears ingested,
hands strong with blood and warm,
certify it will be *fight* today, not *flight*.

But who or what?
Nothing is there.

Shall I fight my financial situation,
injustice, poverty, world problems,
everything not right?
My heart beats now
ready for the crisis.
It is here, I feel it.

I shall predominate,
by God, this time!
I can do it!
I'll fight it!

Where is it?

FEAR DREAM 67

6/67

Castles far away
snugly in the hills,
comfortable, serene,
surrounded by the deepest green,
the strangest green,
near a lake as blue
      or bluer than the sky.

Brilliant noonday sun
fuses all with life.
The birds from tree to tree,
the fox,
the man,

the woman.
Listen carefully.
Hear grass growing,
   breath of trees,
   quiet insistence,
   earth-sound,
   no sound.

Giant hawks!
Black and rough
wings a mile wide,
hurtle on the scene.
Blot out the sky.
Blot out the castle.
Blot out the lake,
the living things.
Paralyzed, I freeze.
Muscles tied, bound,
a thousand cords around.
Fear dream 67.
Hope I go to heaven.

SOUND OF LIFE

12/67

Beyond my window,
open there,
a fine contralto,
voice in tune,
caught the magic edge of sound,
and with an ever-surer grasp,
swelled to her potential;
solid, lasting, musical,

then tapering, full and round,
mellowed on a softer note,
clean and quiet
to the end,
then definitely off.

And so my life,
responding ever stronger
to the steady pull of fate,
runs quickly to the statement,
full and rich,
and then must level off,
quietly fade away.
And, egotistically, I hope
that someone close to me,
(when I'm gone)
will hear my note
softly on the wind
and remember me with love.

THE SEARCH

12/67

For those deficient naturally,
there's nothing but the search.
We read and think and ask ourselves
and analyze the church.

Aha! You say, just stop the search
and then you'll see
you'll have it just like me.

The easy sun will warm your toes

and life will love you as it goes.

I have, at times, stopped the search
and, true, found something there.

Unhappiness in jester's clothes
and staring back with vapid eye.
A blissful world of ignorance
and not a reason why.

There is no doubt,
it's not for me.
Unknowingly, I sigh.

For peace of mind for those unblessed,
the search is grateful, needed rest.

THE AWAKENING

4/73

Awareness flickered faintly
  in the dark behind his eyes
before they opened, greatly,
  to the wonder of the skies.

For the clouds were slowly lifting
  and a vision to behold
with the morning sun behind them
  and their edges flaming gold.

And long he lay transfixed
  absorbing visually there,

for this, his first experience,
  was so wondrously rare.

When swift a rush of wind
  descended light upon his ears
and sound became a vital part
  of all his tender years.

And raptly did he listen
  to the variable breeze
as it hissed along the grasses
  and it moaned between the trees.

And wonderment of sight and sound
  lay rich within his breast
and he exulted in this being
  and felt singularly blessed.

Then soft along the meadow
  wafting sensuous perfumes
rose a languid winding airway
  from the white narcissus blooms
that played about his hair and face
  and lingered in his nose
and swept along the length of him
  before it gently rose.

And consciousness of scent
  arrived and took its rightful place,
a third and mighty tool to serve
  in loyalty and grace.

And teeming was his mind afraid
  to understand his being,

this formidable triumvirate
   of scent and sound and seeing.

But as his comprehension
   was beginning to improve,
there stirred within his body
   a compulsiveness to move.

And blood was full upon his arms
   and strength of leg infused
and neck and chest were charged and taught
   and ready to be used.

And lightly did he lift himself
   and stood himself erect
and nostrils flaring, breathed the air
   and savored its effect.

Notes - Precursors

What is interesting to me is that my first effort unearthed a profound universal dilemma, perhaps the key issue for all mankind: How do we know whether we're living the unconscious life if its chief characteristic is that things seem normal? The world today needs to answer that one for its own survival.

My second effort revealed latent anger, which surprised me at the time. I didn't know I was angry, but here it is, the second poem, *Age of Anxiety*. I struggled with unable-to-be-shared poems until *Fear Dream Sixty-seven* appeared. What are the giant hawks all about? I did have some remote idea as to how I wanted life to be in *Sound of Life*. It's easy to see how my mate should be the one to *remember me with love.* It wasn't happening! Looking for solutions was a state of mind for me late in 1967. Some inner person far below the surface was stirring up the muck, bitterly complaining, as in *The Search.*

Continuing to snooze until 1973, I began to play with what was supposed to be a poem-novel, *The Awakening,* about a healthy young man who wakes up with no memory of things past. I was then supposed to tell the tale of someone who took a fresh look at everything with no prejudices or past qualifying attitudes. I woke him up, but hadn't the foggiest idea of how even to fictionalize a fresh look at things. I think he died the next day.

Six years lumbered past. My three daughters were becoming teenagers, and by 1976, *window ever dirtier,* my personal pain growing like a healthy weed, the seasonal Southern California Santa Ana winds came blowing through and around our house at the mouth of Malibu Canyon.

The Santa Anas are hot, dry desert winds. They can be relentless and annoying for days, and are responsible for the devastating Southern California brush fires. They seem to elicit latent perversions in some people. Riots are prone to break out, arsonists become compulsive and sensitive people become edgy. The Santa Anas were here again and heavily resonating with my own discontent. They swept over like some final provocation and created within me a state of agitated compulsion. I needed to tell somebody *something*, even if only myself, and so began writing in a poetic form whatever occurred to me, unconscious or not.

Part 2 - Agitation

UNTIMELY WIND

Unconfined,
the hot, untimely wind
is whistling through the canyons,
roaring through the trees,
combing the dry grasses,
the brittle chaparral.

Unheeded, she drives,
compulsive and abandoned
toward the sea.
I feel her strength,
her utter freedom
as she sweeps toward the sea.
She must pay an urgent visit
to the surface of the sea.

Unconfined,
the hot, untimely wind
comes whispering, moaning,
comes crying through the grasses,
the blackened chaparral.

Unheeded, she's going.
Abandoned
she's flowing
to the sea.
She bows her head
and pressures
toward the sea.

"WHAT THE HELL AM I DOING HERE?"

1/76

"What the hell am I doing here?"
I take off my shoes
and fall apart.
I drink coffee for lunch,
spill off at the mouth.
And wired for sound,
I start to fly.

Sing all day long
eloquent tunes
of my own genius.

I play the role.
Am daring.
Am dashing.
Am devil-may-care.

'Til I crash,
like now,
with my shoes off.
I fall apart
and ask myself,
"What the hell am I doing here?"

WHERE WILL I GO?

1/76

How am I love?
By lust and here.

What will I can?
I do, I do.
Where will I death?
Will go, will go.

THE ANT AND GOD

I see the ant.
I step over him.
He sees me not,
nor my typewriter,
which I carry.
He hurries,
steadfast,
on his way.

I know God
as the ant knows me,
and my typewriter.

COSMIC CLOCK

In a single tick
of the Cosmic Clock
I'm strata.

I WAIT

My idle hands
are filled with blood.
  My heart beats
  lethargically.
I am lethargic.
  I think,
  not.

I am.
  I know.
  I see.
I feel my fat hand's
  hot blood.

I wait.

I wait in a tiny seat
among thousands,
  my one wish,
  to be alone.

What myriad
series of circumstances,
  agreements,
  commitments,
  habit patterns,
  have produced this bored being?

  This being
  of discontent
  with hot blood hands.

Wishing for aloneness
among thousands.

I wait.

JOHN HENRY

1/76

The clear, cool slicing
of a knowing eye.
The growing trust.
   Oh, for an idea!

To murk along in the sea
beneath the brown waters,
and think that above the glimmering surface,

the sky, clouds, breeze,
   could sweep him into arms of angels.

But, there he is, stuck.
Pinned and wriggling,
squirming like a rat
   impaled on a prong.

And yet, he knows it's there.
He feels its call, its urgency,
it's all life.
But his every effort
   mires his being more deeply.

You know, I know, everyone knows, but John,
   to let go is to live.

To stop the struggle means an upward float.
With great strength and stillness of will,
he ceases to struggle and slowly, meekly,
gently, rises toward the surface,
   the surface and the idea.
Toward the bright light rising,
effortlessly rising,
like a blowfish, brown and prickly,
like a lovely toad ascending
   through the muck.

Like a painted eye with a willingness to open,
he lifts and rises, quiescent, still,
will gently nudge the surface,
and there, as if to see the face of God,
   will dare to look.

From the lethargy of life withdrawn.
From the gnawing apathy he comes
to nudge the surface of the light,
the mind, the vision, the idea.
At the surface, face to face,
and looking only lightly,
for eagerness would blinding be,
destroying his ability,
   to perceive.

And so it passed,
John Henry slowly merged
with flowing grains and window panes
and sunlight on a smiling house
   and children's laughter in the wind.

He came to merge with the living presence,

from the tepid sea arisen,
by welcome *"strangers hands"* uplifted,
came to look at you and me.

NOT POLITE

2/76

At the speed of light
times ten,
the star moves away from me.
Where is it going?
Why so fast?
Why does it go at all?
It should be content
to remain in place
and behave
that I may study it,
take notes,
exhaust its secrets.
I'm not used to
things retreating,
things so big,
things so bright,
things ferocious in the night.
A star should stick around,
keep me company,
advise me when I'm sick,
entertain me when I'm well.
I should take a star for granted,
but it won't let me.
Insists on blazing away
at the speed of light,

burning with the audacity of a million suns,
going to places I'd never go.
Rocketing away
through a frozen night,
not looking back,
not thinking of me,
not polite.

BIRTH

2/76

Still, stillness
breathlessly waiting
space unfilled

purposefully seeded
a resting and freshness.

A stillness of snow
drifted and sloping
a silent glazed surface
a hoping

A cross-threaded web
moves on the wind

silent and floating
awaiting

Shell in a sandstone
locked in the darkness
endlessly waiting
forbearing

A waiting and breathing
silent and living
a purposeful waiting
fulfilling

A stillness and blackness
a warm moonless night
a soft wind a-wafting
a-stirring

Time is for waiting
deciduous tree
content with its juices
abiding

Compulsively beating
a beating with meaning
things in brown mud
wait for bursting

A mild agitation
fluid-like motion
disturbingly strong
fascination

Wind in the willows
rising at night
freshens the leaves
delighting

Discomfort and beating
warm and unseeing
a floating and twisting

and coming to rest
earth's giant cycles
creating the seasons
a cooling and warming
never to rest

A pressure releasing
warmness and weary
progressively urgent
repeating and beating,
anxious, retreating

A squeezing and helplessness
a blazing white light
a freezing white nightmare
a flailing at night
a drowning in sound
a screaming!

ANOTHER DAY

2/76

And so you say
you won't come in,
and I wanting you so
to stay and talk to me,
you refuse with

"Really, I must go.
This splitting headache
hurts me so."

And I,

wanting not to hurt your feelings,
reply, *"Oh, my poor dear kitten,*
may I get you something?"

And then you say,
"Really, no. I must be going.
Thank you for everything.
You've been so kind.
Please, do not walk me to the car.
I shall be fine."

"When will I see you?"
Say I, blurting it out,
looking you in the eyes,
those eyes that once shone so bright
with laughter and life,
now with a tear
just in the corner
and little crinkle lines
of life's concerns.

"Another day," she says
and walks away.
I follow her with my eyes.
Her comely shape,
her corseted thigh,
her white gloved hands
and Sunday hat
held with a pin
and one gray hair,
drifting, astray,
on the wind.
The sound of a motor car
driving off.

And then she is gone.
Silence strikes me, sudden,
as a fall in the night.
I fall into reverie
and memory,
of all the things
she'd meant to me
and all the things
I'd meant to be.
And so,
perhaps it's better this way.
"Another day." she'd said.
Perhaps, again, I say,
"Another day."
I turn and walk back in.

I ROLL A ROCK

2/76

I roll a rock
that would roll on me.
I will prevail,
eventually.

MODERATION

I am not my name.
I am not what I've done.
I am not what I think I'll do.

By the time I say

I am,
I am not.

I walk through space
and step through faith.
I am a process
always in motion,
my grave my destination.

SOMEBODY ELSE

The real me
is somebody else.

EMANUEL

2/76

Leaping from a cloud.
tiny stick-figure
smaller than the sun
gleefully falling,
arms awry,
into another billowy bed?
You're not dead.

EMANUEL!
Come out now.
I see you there,
seaweed in your hair,
playing with seashells
and patterns of sunlight

on jewel-strewn sand
in a saltwater land.

EMANUEL!
Is that you
that I barely see,
through swamp mist,
drifting, silvery,
atop the Cypress tree
beckoning me?

EMANUEL!
Please talk to me.
You with eyes
that see through mine.
You, whose soul
knows all souls.
You, with time
that knows no time.
Tell me I belong to you.
Tell me you love me, too.
Show me again
the variety and range
of what I long to do.

SLEEP

On hands and knees
I creep
through a field
of foolish yellow daisies.

Wild of eye
they gesture,
oblivious to night
in fading light.
Eventually,
I sleep
beneath the stars.

POOR PASSERBY

The leaves, dirt, cinders
tumbled by
blackening
the passerby.

STOPPED BY GLASS

The rain tries to reach me.
Stopped by glass!
Breezes try to teach me.
Stopped by glass!
Birds would like to sing to me.
Stopped by glass!
Bells would like to ring to me.
Stopped by glass!
Guess I'll go outside.

NONSENSE

The rain that strikes my window pane
and following down the glass
to mingle with the flowers
and the flowing grass
can kiss my ass.

MORE NONSENSE

Down the lanes of window panes.
In the store for more.
Down the chute came a boot.
From the shore, the roar.

IMMACULATE

Immaculate
the hearts of angels.
We have time.
Purely sings the winds of ages.
And so is mine.

ON THE RAGGED EDGE

3/76

On the ragged edge
I hold with bleeding nails,

waiting for a change,
from within
or without.
On a razor's edge, I balance,
no shoes, no umbrella.
Were I to stand still,
then, should I be sliced through
as an orange upon a block,
quivering in halves,
double dead.
Perhaps the teeth of gears will snap.
Perhaps a flood will wash us all away.
Perhaps the sun will burn us black.
I wait for the day.

GO FIND YOURSELF

Go find yourself was the word.
Mingle with nature and soak up her soul.
Blend with the landscape as the bird and the deer.
Find what it means to not be yourself.
See what it's like to be part, not the whole.
Time not to be your name.
Time not to be your past.
Time not to do what's expected.
Expect nothing of you,
but see how you flow.
See where you'll go.
Find what you know.

Notes - Agitation

Early in 1976, I was stressed by overwork, our cheerless family situation and poor communication with my spouse. Compassion was non-existent. My wife and I hotly disagreed on methods of raising children and avoided mutual problem solving by escaping into our separate vocations. My *poeticness* was an involuntary response to a critical need for sympathetic dialogue; an instinctively correct response, since effective poetry elicits awareness of feelings, a state I'd blocked for years and one to which it was imperative I return.

The quite unconscious message from *John Henry* was, if I'd just let nature take its course, allow feelings to arise, to *. . . nudge the surface of the light,* things would be fine. The phrase, *Another Day* initiated unmarried life as a possibility, *. . . perhaps it's better this way. Another day.* And *Emanuel* was the first indication of my bright inner spirit awaiting a discovery on my inner person who could show me *. . . the variety and range of what I long to do.*

Next to my office was a dance studio operated by a UCLA graduate student about to get a degree in Dance Therapy. Her thesis was to be on her experiences having led selected adults in six movement therapy classes. Invited, I courageously joined the group of nine. We moved, eyes closed, in contact with one another, we responded to colored lighting, we danced in and out of imaginary spaces, pretended to be born, moved our bodies to love, anger, indifference and verbally shared our feelings. I was being introduced to a different, feeling, side of myself.

The poem *Go Find Yourself* was written after our final class, which was a dawn-to-sunset hike to the top of Boney Ridge, the highest local mountain range. We were not to speak for the entire day or impact nature in any way, but to allow nature its way with us; clouds drifted silently by, the sun moved inch by inch, shadows of leaves rippled, shadings of light richened the landscape, sounds of birds and the breeze in the leaves caressed our ears, and ants, beetles and lizards moved on the earth. I discovered the difference between man-pace and nature-pace. I spent the twilight high on a boulder promontory, watching changing light, alone with a beautiful female person whose serene presence stirred something deep within me I hadn't felt for a long time. The full moon just up, the sun yet setting, the orange, lavender and indigo sky between.

Part 3 - Ruminations

SHORTED OUT

100-watt bulb,
300-watt jolt.
Trembling, I wait
under the lightning bolt.
300-amp jolt,
100-amp capacity.
I hiss and spark
(a waning tenacity)
and flare and smoke.
In the dim-damp-dark,
I rattle my wires
and dance on rocks,
set electric fires:
a low-voltage box,
overloaded by incoming current,
exploded. No doubt,
by overwork, goaded,
shorted out!

MY HOPE

I hope today
to not be me,
valuing, as I do,
anonymity.

LOST SON

3/76

I say to the boy,
"How are you, boy?"
He looks at me
with open eyes
as if to ask,
"Who are you?
and,
"Why do you wish to know?"
I smile an easy smile,
take off my hat,
and with handkerchief
so slightly soiled,
I wipe my brow.
Uneasily, I say,

"You are my own,
the one I love,
the boy I've kept
as part of me
for, lo, these years.
The one I've longed to hold
so close within my arms
until the days and hours
of all the time
whereof we've lost
shall come to catch us
once again
and we are filled to overflowing,
with love, glowing."

He looks to his shoes,

hands shoved in pockets,
shoulders hunched
and then to my face,
again, he says,
"Are you nuts?"

WHAT DO YOU SEE?

4/76

Now that we are alone
and you trust me,
and you have shown me
that you like me,
please sit with me
and let us be together.
                ...
Pleasant, isn't it?
Just you and I
and the setting sun
about to sink beneath the sea?
                ...
Breathe deeply the twilight air
and as the sun's last rays
are just a moment gone,
exhale,
and as you do,
imagine your eyes,
still closed,
on a vertical axis,
turning,
in whichever direction you like,
slowly at first,
in perfect unison,

twirling.
That's right.
Relaxed and alert,
let your eyes in their
whirling
pick up speed.

...

And now they are rapidly spinning,
silently spinning
behind your lids.
Whirling in unison,
perfectly matched,
steady as lead.
Let them spin
for a moment or two.

...

Enjoy it.

...

And now they are slowing.
More slowly they spin.
Silently rotating
ever more slowly.

...

Now they are turning,
as in the beginning,
hardly at all,
relaxed and alert.

...

Enjoy it.

...

When I give the signal to stop
your eyes will click to a stop,
however, instead of you facing them
out to the world,

they will come to a stop
facing in,
into your center,
into the heart and the soul of your being.

STOP!

What do you see?

I see a blackened void
endless in dimension
where nothing will reside.
From my inward looking eyes,
stationary,
unmoving in the darkness,
I step,
as a tiny man,
to explore the immense dark cavern.
Unafraid, I go hunting
with my candle
through the blackness
and the vastness
of the void.

I know there is a something,
some dark secret
somewhere lurking
on the edges of the room.

What's this?

A room of many brown-faced doors,
on the walls, floor, ceiling,
each with jeweled handle thrusting,

inviting me to open.

I try the first.

A shaft of light so blinding
strikes me full upon the face,
it makes me squint.
And then the misty whiteness
of a lonely beach
and fog in wisps and clearing,
sunlight penetrating
to the rippling sand.

I see the frothy tongues
of muted waves
come licking at my toes
and biting me with cold
and in the distance,
out to sea,
I hear a joyful singing
and then the somber ringing
of a low-pitched bell
struck in perfect measured time
and the singing and the bell
in utter contrast mingling.

The song,
a sound of sweetness,
love and joy in living.
The bell,
a doleful measuring
of time going by.

I close the door,

reflecting,
and in a moment,
curious again,
grasp another jeweled handle.

Gently, I open
and look directly into eyes
that look directly into mine.
I see the soul of another being
as that other being searches mine.
We smile.
We cry.
We love.
We walk, hand in hand,
into an unlikely land
where a tree is a tree
and a me is a me.

We ask a bird, *"How do you fly?,"*
and away on the wind he soars.
We ask the bush,
"How do you grow?"
and a flower springs from the bud.
We ask the stone,
"Why do you sit,
heavy, still,
in the heat of the desert day?"
The insect creatures beneath,
stir in the coolness,
awaiting the night.

We lie in the shade
of a pepper grove
on bluffs that fall to the sea

and watch the billowing clouds
drag their rainstorm feet.

We feel the cooler breeze
descending from the trees.
Inhale the dampened freshness
of the eucalyptus leaves.
We hear the pattering sounds
of raindrops on our palms
and fingertips
and taste the droplets
on our lips.

So content we are to be.

A draft, ominous, cold,
from the open door and black beyond,
shatters my serenity.

I step back,
reluctantly,
through the open door
and gently let it close.

Back, again,
within the dimness of my mind,
I select another jeweled handle
and pull it once again.
I become disheartened
by a melancholy room
painted black
yet glowing somber red
and on a flowered platform

stands an open coffin
and a stiffened human form
lying petrified within.

I close the door
and close my eyes.
Unhappily, within my brain,
the dreadful image
I yet retain.

I look for the entrance eyes
and see them as before,
staring blankly in.
As a tiny man,
quickly, I climb out
to daylight,
sanity and fresh air.

BREAK SERENELY ON THE DAY

4/76

The day breaks
serenely.
It is I
who add turmoil
and color it tense.

It doesn't make sense.
I should break serenely
on the day
however it shows,
whether it blows
or rains

or bakes
or snows.

I must learn the way
to break
serenely
on the day.

HENRY, GIVE IT UP

When will Henry give it up?
The lady hasn't gone away.
He handed her the silver cup,
but said she couldn't stay.

RAGGED DAYS

4/76

And then the ragged days
and variety of ways
the Mother Earth will speak.
We will seek to understand the land
and how the windstorm plays
with broken bottles on the sand
and the seagull's beak
and the military band.

I see a mountain peak
and massive rocks
that saw the sky.

I see a cloud that stands on end;
dirigible upended,
sinking through the honeyed air.
I hear an iron bell
tolling out the day
and taste the rain
sticking to my fingertips
with my tongue and lips
and a white-gloved dowager sips
a sugared lemon drink
on the brink of sanity
and vanity
and boredom
and goredom.

THE SECRETS

4/76

Little do they
in the dark of their own ...
knowing what and why,
yet not telling,
or saying
or stating
or communicating
in any way, but,
with serious countenance
and intense thought,
even though ordinary,
or strange,
or, for that matter,
both, even so,
we knew

and we told them,
but they wouldn't.
or couldn't.

even the will-o-the-wisp,
won't.
they could if they tried,
but they don't.
if they were paid,
they would,
but no one pays me
or my family tree.
and so, I sit,
thinking, rocking,

not blaming
or lauding,
but letting the world …
confiding its secrets
to nobody else
but you.

BODY

7/76

Clean cotton shirt. Clean cotton pants.
Clean body, fine body, lean body, fits in my clothes.
I lie still, refreshed and feel good in my body.
I feel nothing but warmth and contentment
    as my bright blood flows its effortless way.
It visits my toes and heart and hands.
I tingle with health.
It feels good to live here.

I love it here.
I wear clean, fine fitting clothes
    of skin, muscles, guts and bones.
    I like it here.
I could live here always.
I am at home in my body.
This is where I live,
fully oxygenated with relaxed muscle tone,
    not hungry or thirsty or out of breath,
    not needing of elimination, not gurgling
    or inwardly working, not gaseous
    or nauseous or overeaten of useless foods.

I lie on my bed a mass of living cells,
meat and bone with emotions,
brain, senses, and a miraculous body
built for anything I want to do.
Content, un-hurting,
I love it here.
This is where I live.
I shall stay here until I die.
I don't want to leave.

LATE AFTERNOON

7/76

The sun feels good on my skin. It makes it glow. It draws it out. I soak up vitamin D. When I turn on my side, the sun warms me. It sends loving rays to wash my body. Laving rays, yellow and gold, shimmering down, playing on my back and thighs, warming my buttocks through my swimsuit. The light from the sun plays about the sand and towel, my hat. It heats my glasses frames. Effortlessly, my watch ticks. I relax. I doze. The striving goes from my body. My lids are heavy and I drift and dream. My finite thoughts turn infinite. I am logical in my thinking until, dimly aware, I'm not logical at all, I fall into sound sleep and the golden, laving, loving sun's rays play on my back and the sun moves a noiseless notch to the west and I do not perceive that it does so, for I am no longer present. I am repairing my body. My heart is lightly stroking, sending warm blood to repair, maintain, wash and clean and I am unaware and do not exist . . . I stir with a cooler breeze that cools my side. I sleep on. I awaken, cold. The sun, farther in the west, has slipped behind a cloud. The golden rays no longer dance upon my skin. In place of the rays, a playing breeze eddies in the hollows and contours of my body. Goose bumps raise on my arms, back and thighs. It is time to leave. My skin is both burnt and cold. I wipe the sand from my legs, stomach, chest and pick up my towel. I leave, feet in the cooling sand.

RAIN

7/76

By an open window, sleeping, content, smiling, I sleep on. By the open window, I wait for rain. I know it's coming. I smile and wait, warm, snug, protected and content, having been tucked in and kissed. Smiling, I close my eyes and wait for rain. The wind has been strong, but now it is still, hushed, expectant, and then a cooler rush of wind and thick droplets pad the sill, leaves, grass. The sound on the roof is bliss. I relax, warm, snug, kissed and content. I sleep and the rain spatters the window sill and onto my smiling face. I hear thunder rolling through the heavens, and a lightning flash brightens the lids of my eyes, and the rain, renewed, splatters, ever more sharply on the sill, and tiny droplets are on my peaceful, sleepy, smiling face. It rains with a rush, now intense. The air is thick with raindrops slanting into the yard, leaves, roof, earth. The heart of the rain and the cool wind are upon me now, and I am secure in my bed, perfectly sheltered by the close overhead roof and its roar and the gutters are spilling and rivulets in the grass have formed and are draining and I doze and smile and soon the heavens lighten again and the thunder booms through the clouds, again, and I sleep, contented, warm, relaxed, smiling, kissed, loved and sheltered through the long night rain.

I AM

8/76

I am
I hear
I see
I feel
I have energy
I have latent energy
   my energy waits
I reign it in
I do not release it
I am filled with it
   to the brim
I save it
My heart beats quietly
   solemnly
   waiting
   powerfully
capable of delivering
all the *'I am'* there is -
   soon.

I SHALL BURST

I am charged and ready to burst.

Like a Fourth of July bomb,
I wait, wick extended,
ready for lighting.

Silently, I walk,
cool air in my nostrils.

My feet are cold,
the stars unusually bright.
I look for Mars.
I do not think,
yet feel my thoughts.

I am.
I wait, discontented.
I'd like to lose myself in running.
Run for a hundred miles
through twilight, night and dawning.
Then exhausted,
 I would fall beneath a Sumac,
lost, and sleep an eternity.
My energy is boundless,
yet I do nothing.
I am hostile. I am strong.
I am frustrated. I am belligerent.
My fathomless energy seems futile,
though it is where I live.

I wait for the right time.

Charged and ready,
I wait for the proper moment.
I wait for the gears of the world
and the signs of the Earth to adjust.

Then, shall I burst.

THIRD BRAIN DOWN

8/76

Deep in the deep.
Deepest - deeper,
Thinking, third brain down.
Thinking deep with feeling.
Feeling deep with thinking.
All of a piece.
Energetic lethargy,
Super-concerned
And solid,
Like thick, tough meat,
I think-feel,
And feel-think.
I feel what I know,
Deeply, deepest,
Deeper,
Third brain down

STROBOSCOPE

Shot by a stroboscope
in each bright posture,

in every nuance
and gesture, I'm seen.

I dance in space
and the flashing light,
in measured time,
catches my life
in angular attitudes

I SIT IN BETWEEN

8/76

I sit in between
wanting and caring
hoping to shed some light
hoping to guide
  to teach
  to show the way
in some slight quandary
ready to speak my mind
should I find the way
  the proper time
  the place
and what attitude should I assume
and what attitude shall I find dear children
  I want more than anything
  for you to take joy
  in being you

BAOBAB

The Baobab sucks
at the juice of my life.
It has rooted my planet
through lack of attention.
I must dig it out
whatever the cost,
and when it is gone,
plant flowers and fruits
and pay more attention.

PLANTING SEEDS

12/76

If I plant a seed
a plant will grow
and bear a fruit
which I may eat.

It is prudent
I do not plant
a bitter seed.

CARING

The Universe
is incapable
of worry,
and, therefore,

cares not what I do.

I, of course, care.

HEAVEN

I climbed the highest pinnacle
and leaping, rent the clouds
to peer at blue-black heaven
and a single, brittle star.

EDGE OF THE DEAD

2/77

To live in a world
of quivers and gurgles
of clackings of bones
and movings of juices
and nails dug deep in the dirt.

To live in a world
of monotonous heartbeats
alone in a blackness

of cycling passions
and effortful strivings
lost in the midst of the earth.

To inhabit a bed
at the edge of the dead
alive without knowing you live.

A cog in a scheme
in a nameless dream
unable to weep,
in a lethargy
not quite sleep.

WAITING FOR A DAUGHTER

2/77

Twinkling tones of tear-shaped glasses
brighten the eyes of the local lasses.

A steaming volcano of vegetable soup.

Simple salt and pepper twins
with silver heads and finger holes.
Someone sorting silverware
and napkin-covered rolls.

An ice-cold cracker in a crinkly wrapper.

   "Basically, I believe..."
The rippling song's refrain,
   "I wish you wouldn't leave..."
My effort all in vain.

Table tops in tile shimmer in the sun.

A kerosene lamp
with a petrified wick.
An empty bowl
and a sandwich stick.

A single yellow jonquil listens to my heart.

An elemental shape,
cool and smooth to touch.
Oh, my darling daughter,
I love you very much.

THE ANSWER

4/77

I have a book called *The Answer*,
   but I never read it.
It lies on my desk in the corner.
It gathers dust.
The jacket curls.
I long to know what's in it,
   but I never once have reached for it.

At night, sometimes, I cannot sleep.
My head spins.
I try to think things out.
I am thoroughly at a loss.
Straws on the wind,
   leaves on the tide.

My answer book lies, inert,
   on the corner of my desk,
     lent by a well-meaning friend.

Its cover bears the title,
   The Answer.
It will explain everything fine
that I need to know.

And, I desperately need to know.

When I complain,
   as I usually do,
   my friend says,
"Please open the book."
   The Answer.

I always plan to.
I *"plan"* to right now.
When my mood strikes me right.
When the stars are aligned in a beautiful design.
When the moon whispers to me during an eclipse.
When night winds promise rain
   on the 5th of December.
I do have the answer in my personal possession.
It's in that book, there by the door,
   The Answer,
all of it written,
what I'm going to know.

I have never reached for it.
At times I do not think I see it.

Perhaps I don't want
   my friend's answer.
His may be dull.

What if mine were
   a rampageous river
   begging to be followed
   up the frigid canyons,
   in the hollows of the turns,
   through the mountains

and the meadows,
bright with flowers.

The answer book's a thief;
robs me of discovery.

I must learn not to ask
for what I don't want to know.

DREAM, DISCOVERY, INSIGHT

4/77

My newly tanned face
came off in my dream.
I reached at the hairline and pulled at the skin.
The skin and my face peeled slowly away.
First one side,
carefully, slowly,
I peeled it back.
Beneath was a new, clean, younger skin;
a new person, me, with shining eyes.

I pulled at the top of my scalp.
I peeled the skin off my face,
slowly, deliberately, until it all came off
like a long, limp mask with hair attached.

As I held it to show a horrified friend,
it became repulsive, rotten;
a ghastly, detached mask
with holes for eyes, mouth and nose.

I looked at my face in the mirror.

It was black, diseased.
I was afraid.

I reached to pull the black skin off.
My chin crumpled like black cottage cheese
  and threatened to fall to the floor.

I peeled again at my hideous mask
  and pulled it once more away.
In the mirror, this time,
  a new face with healthy, pink skin,
  eyes black and shining
  and hair glistening,
  greeted my eyes.
Astounded, I gazed at my own new face,
  different from the old.
  My own new self.

I DRIFT IN A WAKING DREAM

9/77

I drift in a waking dream.
I walk with my heart.
  I glide in cool shadows
  of roses and ferns.

I leap to clouds
  and descend, a fluttering rain,
  born on the down
  of a delicate air.
A welcome storm
  with fragrance
  rich as my love.

I sweep the grass
  of a quiet valley
  and merge in delight
  with tall, green shoots.

I trickle and run,
  swirl and tumble.
I play with clarity,
  light
  and jewel-like stones.
I run to the sea
  and merging,
  drift in a waking dream.

Notes - Ruminations

The student teacher completed her thesis and I continued subsequent classes with her, as did my newly discovered woman friend. The weekly improvisational movement classes provided a means of releasing suppressed feelings and allowed a safe social contact with all females around whom I'd always felt inept.

My spouse seemed pleased I was enjoying the classes and even came to several sessions, however, I felt her critical presence as an intrusion into my personal space. I didn't see her as resonating with the basic therapeutic principles underlying our activities. Group members were to be accepted and affirmed just as they were and their ideas or ways of moving were not to be judged, criticized, corrected or manipulated in any way. This movement expression class ended upon the tragic and untimely death of the original teacher. It was, however, almost immediately resumed by someone of equal motivation and creative ability, and the weekly dance experience under the new *Teach* was to play a powerful role in my personal growth for 12 years.

Meanwhile, I continued my poetic endeavors. *Shorted Out, Ragged Days,* and *I Shall Burst* attest to feelings of overwork, discontent and frustration. In *What Do You See,* I find a sense of urgency. a soul mate, and a worrisome look at death, in *Body, Late Afternoon* and *Rain,* I explore three areas of safety, used in these days to provide balance to my considerable tensions. The two most significant poems in this series are *Lost Son* and *Secrets.* In 1976, the concept of *'inner child'* was not publicly prevalent nor one with which I was familiar. Yet in *Lost Son,* here he is with a semi-formal, stuffy old gent *(a later me)* making awkward overtures to him. *Secrets* told me I was withholding information needing to be revealed.

In January of 1977, I was invited by my woman friend and her husband to make plans for an addition to their house for a playroom and art studio. I hesitated several weeks before accepting, because I knew my friend and I would be brought into necessary and welcome contact by the needs of the project, which would only inflame my desire for her company. I assented, and in October, the project almost completed, we found ourselves miraculously and ominously in love. I wrote *I Drift in a Waking Dream.* Our lives and marriages were to be irrevocably changed.

Part 4 - Dilemma

CHANGE

12/77

Change has me from the inside.
It's been coming long,
like growth of moss
on cypress trees
or coral rocks
in southern seas.

I'm filled with change
like a beaker of steam.

It flows behind my eyes and mouth.
It penetrates my bones and skin.
It infiltrates each nerve and vein.
It rules me from within.

I cough mist
and wisps curl from my nose.
like silent spiral ghosts.

But change to what?

SEEDS OF MYSELF

12/77

Soft my wind
that loves the fields
comes airily through my face.
I'll forget my race with ghosts of beings
wishing they were me.

I must be free
to live in a land
of color and line
as rich as my dream;
to ride on a musical beam
as bright as the joy in my heart
and listen to rhymes
of dandelions
in the warmth of a mid-spring day;

to play in between
Venus and Moon
and ride on the back
of a fearful night;
(It is my right.)

To love the face
and thoughtful grace
of a woman who's much like me,
so the tree of my being
shall bear sweet fruit
and the seeds of myself
take root.

UNDECIDED

2/77

The river, slowing,
comes to an uncertain stop;
threatens to tip and flow backward.

The air is stiff.
A branch doesn't move.

A bubble doesn't burst.

A baby's breath of wind
tickles the sky and clouds
painted on the surface,
but has no effect.

The sun smiles grease.
The trees hang limp.
A fisherman sucks his breath.
The weight of the river is balanced,
nervous, threatening,
undecided.

CORRECT AND TRUE

Correct and true,
permanent unshakable love,
sweet solid love,
flows through your sweet body,
generating a binding energy,
that, flowing, returns
and binds my own.

MING AND MANG

12/77

Mang is huge with fire for eyes,
with stones for feet
and hooks for hands.
He walks on tree-stump legs

and slices clouds
with a black-night sword.
Ming, with armored jaw
and iron-spiked toes,
presses them deep
in the river's mud.
His passions in cycles,
weak as a willow,
   strong as a storm,
   awaits the attack.
Mang advances, sword held high.
Ming awaits, afraid to die.
The clatter of battle
shatters all peace.
   The Sun hangs limp,
   The Moon is red,
   the flowers in the fields are dead.
And the blood of Mang
and the blood of Ming
mingle in a thick-snake stream,
that, writhing, burns to the sea
where the surge and pull
of deep-cut currents
scatter it, red, to every shore
for all the world to see.
   The living nations hands,
   with black-knit gloves,
   clasp their bloodied eyes
   and place their leaden skulls
   between their useless thighs.
And then, when eternities have passed,
on some witless, arbitrary day,
the Sun, returning full and round,
casts a healing ray,

separates the two,
declares a fighting stay.
   Mang, half-dead, lies in blood.
   Ming, half-alive, crawls away.
Vivid in parting,
the memories of pain
do not last,
and are all in vain.

MY HEART SANG YOUR SONG

12/77

I missed you today,
but my heart sang your song.
It said,
   you are my pal,
   my buddy,
   my counterpart found,
   my final friend.
To think we have existed
   on parallel courses
   through all these years.
   If only I'd known.
I feel chosen as the special one,
   selected for another chance,
   released, unexpected
   and allowed to return
   as from a distant war.
      My soul mate,
      my mirror image,
      my very own beauty,
      to hold,
      to love.

It is with you
I wish to share
the vitality of my years,
for I only live when you are near.
   I long for you.
   I am lonely for you.
   I want you.
I must fill my empty space with you,
for when you are gone,
   I'm not whole.
      My own.
      My true love.
      My life.

To be with you
   is to have a growing love.

My heart was wound tight
   with many strings
   for many years.
You have released me
   with but a single tug.
I love your eyes,
      your lids,
      your lashes.
I love your fingertips and toes
   and the nape of your neck.
They are made for me to kiss.
   I want you.
   I long for you.
   I love you.

ON BEING FREE

2/78

I run through forests
   racing trunks
   on needles
   soft as down.

I leap branches,
   jump streams,
   hurtle stones.

I run with perfect ease
   and grace,
   in perfect time
   and perfect rhythm,
for I am a man with
   a perfect purpose.

I am clouds and sky,
   wild yellow roses
   in tall green grass,
a lover of food and sleep,
   women and song.

I run like the wind
   combing the field
   on some black night.

I am infinite variety;
   leaves on the tree,
   feathers on the wing,
   scales in the murk
   of some lost sea.

I never stop inhaling.
 My lungs are big as buildings.
 I only breathe out when I want
 and that for purest pleasure.

I am big and free,
 long of arm,
 long of torso,
 hip and thigh.

I swim oceans,
 climb mountains.
I fly through the air
 and sing with birds.

I love it here.
 It's made for me,
 my world.
 It has infinite variety.

I rise and float.
I sing a two-day song.
I play for as long as a year,
 if I want,
and never get tired.
I am a meteoric boulder,
 pea-sized,
tumbling in a shallow stream.

I lie in wait for a year
 or doze and dream
 perfectly content.

Darkness doesn't bother me,

nor does the desert air.

Mighty rainstorms are my home.
I wish they'd never end,
    for I have time.

I do not age,
    but seemingly grow younger
    with every passing day.

The pathway clears itself before me.
Giant pines move their trunks
    to avoid my stride.
Mountains open as I approach,
    and when I'm gone,
    close themselves behind.

I wade the seas
    and visit islands.
The sea turtle is my friend.
    We swim together,
    arm and fin,
    in silent harmony.

I follow the whale
    to hidden depths
    and linger just a while.

I sift my fingers
    through the silts of ages
    in the pitch of the Japanese trench.

I calibrate the shifts
    of continental plates

before I go to lunch.
I marvel at a grain of sand
glistening in the sun.
Or a quiet tear.

Or a drop of dew.
Or a raindrop,
cool and clear.

I love my private world
and my perfect purpose.
The purpose of being.

WITH APOLOGIES TO T. S. ELIOT

"But though I have wept and fasted, wept and prayed,
Though I have seen my head (grown slightly bald)
 brought in upon a platter,
I am no prophet – and here's no great matter;
I have seen the moment of my greatness
 hold my coat and snicker,
 And in short, ..."
(Check which)

_____I was afraid.

_____I was not afraid.

DESPERATE

I am desperate
to tell my stories.
To share a me,
I, only, know.
I am desperate to live
by telling
the moments of my great events,
however small.
I am desperate to see
seeds of my unique tree
grow, startling, to maturity.

I am desperate,
too, to listen
to stories no one else can hear.
To see the richness
of another's *"great events."*

The ones that pass in grayish light,
but in the telling,
told with passion,
come to life
in red and green and white.

I am desperate to tell,
and after telling,
desperate to be told.

OH ANGUISH

2/78

Oh, anguish
   on letting you go.
Your own sweet body,
   so used to mine.
Your breasts and hips,
those loving thighs,
those feet I've held in mine,
   the full, ripe flow
   of your loving form
   I know like my soul.
How can I let you go?
   Discard that smile,
   those eyes that loved me,
   (love me?)
through laughter and spice
   of an eager, early life,
through anguished nights
   of our children's years,
   (and fears)
through buildings and songs,
through fire and rainstorms,
   and myriad ways
   of our sunlit days.
We lived as a key in a lock
   our allotted time.
How can I let those wistful eyes
   fade into mist and time?
I love you
   as my feet firmly planted,
   as I breathe,
   as I see,

as I feel my heart,
    heavy at the thought
    of letting you go.
Oh, anguish!

CAN YOU LET ME GO?

2/78

Can you let me go
    into the land
of my own love?
Land I have never seen
    except in dreams.
Land I have longed for
    through these long years
    as I long for my fingers
    and my eyes.
The soft, brown,
    precious
    eyes of a gentle dog.
Can you let me
    go to my love
as the eye of the dog
    is loved,
is precious to him?
Can you keep me
    from my eye, my love,
when I long to see
    as I long for my hands?
Can you let me find
    my life's longing
in this, my later life
    and the backs

of my wrinkled hands?
Can you let me
   be in that state
you say you've had
   for, lo, these years?
May I find my only love,
   while yet there's time;
to live in the land
   of my loving self?
To sing the song
   I have longed to sing,
for just this once,
   in these final years?
To find my longing.
To find my life.
To find that love,
   heavy upon me?
That love so long overdue,
   overripe, so long,
so longing for use?
Can you find
   in your own true heart
the strength, the love
   to open the gate?
   To let me run
in the grass, hills,
   trees, love
of a later life?
   I would love you so.

I SEE YOU TRY TO HEAL MY HEART

I see you try to heal my heart,
　my heart now laid so bare.
My wound, however, will not close,
　but gapes upon the air.

NO!

A day or two ago,
about to make love,
I asked,
"Please, leave your necklace on?"
(The one I gave you)
"nothing else"
So lovely,
so enticing,
so rich and desirable,
so loving.
You said, *"No!"*
(without a thought)
and took it off,
afraid you'd break it.

IN DEADLY EARNEST

In deadly earnest
I play with lives.
I dangle them on my string.

Solemnly,
I watch them take me in,
   their loving eyes,
   their wistful eyes,
   their laughing eyes,
their crying eyes,
and I, with serious countenance,
telling myself
I long for truth,
blunder my way;
push my white tendril up
through crumbly earth
disturbing rocks,
sand and shiny pebbles,
   awkward,
   ugly,
   wandering,
wondering how I shall get through
   to real growth.
When shall I get
   a new green leaf;
   my first?
This rooting takes so long.
I must live through this period
   with patience,
   frustration,
   longing,
fear for myself,
fear for others.
I must get through this rooting
before I can grow with ease.

MORE OF THE SAME

5/78

Green and black,
tough, gnarled bark trunks
waited like space
and moons flashed.
Roulette wheel moonlights
dazzled beings, who,
dizzy with birthing,
loving and dying,
passed through irrevocable time,
until, at last,
that false hope,
still breath,
pinpoint
arrived with pomp,
heralding repetition.
Beginnings and endings
    merged
and momentary eyes and heads
recognized that
a finite state is illusion
    and that
true God everlasting
    is more of the same.

FLOWING AND SINKING

5/78

Flows and sinks,
rises,
then flowing again

and sinking.
Undulating.
As gray fish,
white stripe,
black, yellow,
pancake eye
stares and leans
on thick, still, water;
element of tube-like rushes,
submerged,
slim as trees,
vertical, and fish,
motionless,
green and growing,
making vertical space,
cool and clear.
Perpendicular the rushes
and motionless, between,
turns with a jerk,
red eye, black fin,
silver stripe.
A curious look.
A lightning jerk.
A darting.
Stillness and floating,
curiosity, inward.
Feeling cool
with juices flowing,
gases bubbling.
Life and striving,
effortlessly rising,
flowing,
sinking.

NOW, IN DARK SHADOWS PLAYING

Now
in dark shadows playing,
light and shivering
the infinite wind
crossing limitless space
infiltrates, fills
lifts and settles
'til brittle night
closes, turns the key
and sadness descending
all the while
graceful, gliding,
lifting, settling,
comes irrevocably
to stillness;
allows motionlessness
to become the leaves,
the dark shadows
light and quivering.

POUNDING

5/78

Lead-heavy hands
pounding with purpose,
with rage, with anguish.
A blood-crammed heart,
a ramrod spirit
and a soul with a promise.
It shatters the still,

thick-shadowed,
cool earth,
with a promise.
A pounding in concert
with fist and heart
in rhythm and blood,
and beats to the stomach rage
fouled with green.
A wounded soul
that pounds with purpose
and knowing and working it out
and going along and letting it out.
A continuous process.
A running the course.
A thundercloud sounding.
A tree trunk pounding.
A finishing out.
A dying away.
A missed beat falling.
A heartbeat stalling.
An ice blue knot
    melting to red.
A lagging of pounding.
A falling, a sobbing.
A stopping.
A sobbing.

EMERGING

Emerging from the grass,
dark, it moved,
uncertain, the grass,
tall, green, unsteady,
then shifting,
a pawn in the wind.
It moved in the dark,
as stars,
piercing the back of the night,
punctured the violet drop.
The green grass glowing,
illuminated from within,
spent its iridescent force,
wavering, then blowing,
steady, then bending,
flowing, then stopping
in the cool night wind.
And emerging there from,
furry and black
with soft yellow eyes
and curved black claws,
vicious, yet gentle,
but fearful,
the creature came forth,
and moving and twitching the grass,
made its meticulous way
into the violent night.

Notes - Dilemma

Our home continued to be chaotic, unpredictable and discontented. In 1978 the differences in life outlook between the parental leaders of the family undermined the confidence of the offspring that anyone was in charge, and the argumentative family atmosphere was ill-suited to peace in the household and the raising of three self-congruent daughters. To make matters worse, I was cheating on my wife, preoccupied about it and distressed. The dream of a compassionate, loving and creative household didn't match the reality. ... *my window, ever dirtier* was causing *the pain to make me clean* ... It was necessary I *scrub* if only *'til pain was bearable again.* With encouragement of my new friend, I entered weekly sessions with a Marriage, Family and Child Counselor intern at the Xavier Clinic in Santa Monica.

During this era of beginning therapy, a large photomural of two oriental warrior puppets in mortal combat hung on the wall opposite the foot of our bed. The suggestion it was better suited elsewhere was met with rebuke and I yielded to keep peace. Though a powerful artwork, the disturbing subject matter inserted itself daily into my viscera and eventually it became the symbol of our relationship: see the poem, *Ming and Mang.* The love poem, *My Heart Sang Your Song,* written directly thereafter, set my two strongest feelings side-by-side as if for some ultimate comparison. This happened unconsciously again in *Desperate,* followed by *Oh, Anguish.*

In the meantime, I longed to be unrestrained in *On Being Free*. I knew my actions were affecting others in *In Deadly Earnest,* and yet I knew it was I who must be saved. This was being accomplished all too slowly in therapy. I had always believed the quotation, *'To thine own self be true.'* But now, my ambivalences blatantly showing, I didn't know to which self to be true. I felt pulled in every direction by a web of forces; my complex work life involving up to eight clients and three draftsman, fatherly duties to three daughters, two relationships, and my need for private time and therapeutic work. The answer lay in finding *'self,'* whatever that was, and I began seriously looking inside. After six months, *Flowing and Sinking* came forth, which has this inward-looking quality, and then an inkling of hope in *Emerging.* Was it self?

Part 5 - Risking

OVER AND UNDER

When will the . . .
in the time of the oval shaped moon,
edge dipped in blood and swollen,
let out the stars,
in their infinite right,
to spread, engulfing,
proclaiming, encompassing?
And when they have found
and permeated
and infiltrated and claimed,
then the right is theirs
and theirs, alone,
and they remain solid,
immovable,
and glow with certainty
unequalled by men.
They are.
They claim.
They do.
For the stars are of the earth,
and none can dig under,
for they are under
as well as over,
and it would do us well
to ponder this thing
and take heed
and absorb this absolute fact
into our beings,
so that none can dig under us,
for we, also, are under
and over if once we see stars
as they truly are.

WHISTLING

Whistling, he goes,
for he is sun
and barefoot on the earth
and rolled jeans
and tanned body
and he walks
and is under the wind
   as well as the rain
and is soaked,
    but never is wet,
    for he claims his space.
He knows, as the wind,
that the tree,
in its solid-state root,
can reach to the pits of the earth
and strike to the sun as well,
and fill every void,
and claim.
    For, it is.
    And, he is.
    And, both are,
    and will be
    and have been
    and so shall we,
    if we do.

GREEN STICK TREE

5/78

Deeply, I deep.
Here in the land
of one lost leaf
and amber sky,
lost in infinity's desert,
tired, looking for . . .
With hope,
I merge with the . . .
and tingle and sleep,
and the great white dove,
wings outspread,
hangs in the sky
and will not speak,
but with loving eye.

I have entered here,
brought to this place,
and I like myself
and this in-between,
for over the mountain
is the land of my dream.

I walk with hope
and the iron-black crows
with hard, yellow eyes
and insulting calls,
unsettle me, now,
though I shall prevail
and move beyond
the green-stick tree
with buds all around.

I CLAIM IT MINE

6/78

I have a . . .
and the solid,
too, too heart
of the wood-nut tree,
spread, as if to the wind,
and growing,
claimed its space,
as a giant hand
clasps the clouds
and wrings them dry
with the certainty of giants
striding in the wood.
Then, as if to . . .
and the heaving
and swelling night
and the coming and going
of the multi-colored stars,
the wind shifting
and sweeping,
slowing, then swooping,
the bird on the wind,
wings outstretching and black,
steady,
yet arching in strength,
moving, as lead,
broadly across the paper,
speeds through the heavens
and marks it mine.

MUSIC TALK

6/78

The sounds reach me.
They have been traveling
from the opposite face of the earth,
and I hear them,
for my eardrums are sensitive
and pick the vibrations
from the stillness of the night.
They tell me that . . .
and I answer them
and they reply
and I listen carefully
and we communicate,
for we are one with the other
and love conversation.
Sometimes we sing to each other
and the music,
to and fro,
crowds the airways.
Sometimes we weep
for the beauty of the sound,
for our listening is . . .
and must be done,
if we are to know.

RARE GIFT

6/78

For, in the beginning
it was this way,
    when,

upon bending closely to the ground
and listening
to tall grass,
   earth,
   dead leaves
   and worms,
the heart, the center,
throbbing powerfully,
let me know that . . .
and, I believed it
and raised my eyes to the blue heavens
and saw the clouds parting
and one lone star,
brighter than Venus,
shone upon me
and said to me,
"You have been.
You are.
You shall become,
before you die."
I kissed the earth
and wept
for this gift of love,
for never before have I . . .
but always have I wanted . . .
So rare is it, that . . .
I need.
I want.
I love.

WINNIE

Winnie is a dog.
Do you love Winnie?
Yes.
Does Winnie love you?
Yes.
Is Winnie a lucky dog?
Yes.
Winnie, big, black,
clear yellow eyes
that burn into your own.
Intelligent, sensitive.
Strength to range a thousand miles.
Lies under the bed
   all day long.
A pat in the morning,
good dog, nice dog.
A pat in the evening,
nice dog, good dog.
And the hours slip by,
minute by minute,
thick as incense
through the long afternoon.
A pat in the evening.
Good dog.
A pat in the morning.
Nice dog.

Winnie broke loose.
Through tall sage
and greasewood
she bounded,

hot on the trail.
Tail up, nose down,
she followed the ground.
Then half-mile away to the Center
to play by the swings,
scuff sand with the children.
Then half-mile away to the creek
she sloshed through bulrushes,
algae and mud.
She lapped the clear water
and went for a swim,
her powerful muscles
glistening in the sun.
A good shake, head, body, tail,
then through a field of flowers
and on to the road where
someone passing found her, lost,
and phoned her in.

Guilt-ridden Winnie,
picked up in the car.
    Shame!
Into the house
with the dog door shut.
And the heavy afternoon
under the bed.
The dozing,
the stretching,
the yawning,
the yearning.
A pat in the evening.
Good dog, nice dog.
And slow clocks tick.
And restless dreams.

And laboring through the night.
Oh, lucky, lucky Winnie.
Oh, lucky dog.

For whom is the dog?

THANK GOD FOR THE DOVE

6/78

Why should I,
when the wind blows high
and the beetle,
with steady stride,
crosses the lonely path.
For as he goes,
so go I.
And the black crow
sits on the pole
and laughs at me
and mocks me
and throws javelin spears
and insults and stones,
and jeers at me.
And over my shoulder,
I look at him
with jaundiced eye
and think, yes, I know,
you're here to stay,
but so is the dove.

LUCKY ONE

6/78

Now and again, the . . .
but, I don't mind.
And having smile,
the sun, the moon,
the mountains green,
the birds, the bee,
the cigarette tree
and the myriad
that cross my mind
with each second's look,
    I do have.
And am the lucky one
when all is said and done.

SCREW

6/78

The screw,
wooden, large threads,
used for courage
as in, *"Screw up your courage."*
I did.
I twisted and turned,
tightened and wept,
twisted again,
'til exhausted and blistered,
I finally succeeded
in turning off love.
And so I have lived
with the pressure up high
and my valve,

through my effort,
has yet remained shut.
Now rusted and shut.
Not a trickle of love
has escaped,
have I loved.
And now, yet alive,
under the speeding arch,
sputtering arteries
splitting with strain;
valves of my heart
yielding in pain,
do I look for a way,
am desperate to know
how to loosen the screw,
how to open the gate,
let love flood out.
I know my mistake.

STONE

6/78

The stone
lies on the desert sand,
freckled, silver-gray,
with watermelon shape.

Quietly, heavily, it sits
with infinite patience,
through the long minutes,
hours, years of our lives,
absorbing sun's rays,
stingingly hot on top,

cool below and dark.

And when the sun has set
and innumerable stars
claim the night sky
and the cool desert wind
whispers low on the sand,
the stone,
quietly radiates heat.
And living things
gather near
to receive the gift of warmth,
the energy from within.

The mother stone,
inscrutable, unfeeling,
yet not without feeling,
lies immobile but alive,
steadfast, unfailing,
content in just being
the stone.

THE JOKE'S ON US

6/78

When yellow dog's teeth
split iron rails
and lightning wracks the eye
and pines and willows scream in the gale.
When the rain splits the window pane
and enters like sperm
impregnating the unthinkable,
then shall blue faces

glow like ugly masks
in the black window
of eternal night
and slack-mouthed,
ragged-toothed,
evil laughter shall abound,
but emit no sound,
for the mask is mute,
and we are deaf,
and the joke is death,
and belongs on us.

I KNOW ME?

6/78

Up from the stomach,
let it emerge.
   I think hard
   and see gray nothing,
   but feel intensely.
I shall be pliant,
   patient,
   nurturing.
I live inside
and it tells me what;
   but not in words.
Its messages come;
Jackal in a sheep's disguise,
dark clouds hiding sunny skies.
   Nevertheless,
I will decipher,
for I know me,
even if I don't.

WHERE SHALL WE GO?

Honey rays pouring,
flowing thickly
over the brim.
And where shall a poor mind go
when there is no thought?
Wind scatters to sea.
Stone lies on sand.
For I am the only one.
And I am the lonely one.
Cat sleeps in grass.
Moon sleeps in sky.
Where shall I go
if I'm not with me?

MOON SHATTERED

6/78

Moon shattered in three.
Grass shadows lay wrinkled
on midnight sand.
Wolves howl in forgotten woods.
When will the . . .
have mercy on me?
April is the violet month.
March is the violent month.
The man with the coat
had no face.
Love becomes the little child.
Shall I win my race?
She whispered in the hall.

Highway noises and crickets.
   I may be late,
   save me a ticket.
She flickered an eyelid
   and stuttered.
No one knows me,
   not even myself.
Cat's tail hangs
   on the lone pine tree.
April is the month of promise.
Rain has no peer.
My father is dead,
   but not in my heart.
I'll love when I do
   or I won't.
Stay with me, fair one.
I know her,
   but she doesn't know me.
Race car drivers
never drink beer. I know my place,
but I'm not here.
When will the yellow flower
   dip its head and drink water?
Train whistles
   frighten the night.
Where do beetles go to sleep?
Roots join hands,
   bow their heads
   and pray.
I'll be a tree
   instead of a me.
She sang a midnight song
   then gave it to me,
      free.

ANGELS SING SWEET SONGS

6/78

First me, then we.
This path will do.
   In the mist and clearing,
   the dead branch silhouette.
Everywhere the song.
Night-birds cry
   then spin their heads.

First the thunder,
   then the rain.
Closed eyelids, smoothed brow.
   My heart shows teeth
   in a smile.
I love to love.
Fourteen hundred elephants
   and not a blade of grass.
The willow tree
   swayed in the breeze.
Yellow dogfish,
   bright black eyes.
   Ripples and swirls
   in still water.

Frogs swim under,
   webbed feet trailing.
I drink with my eyes.
White clouds, blue sky
   reflected in still water.
Seaweed holds water
   so it cannot move.
Angels sing sweet songs.

THE HEARTSORE

6/78

And once dragged from its hiding place,
we see its countenance, weak, slithery,
   frightened of the bright lights,
   fearful, ugly in the sun,
   out of place and unable to return.
What shall we do with it?
What will it do by itself?
It is lost. It is big.
It needs care and feeding.
   It seems to have weight and mass,
   but no sense about how to cope.
It must be dried, spoon-fed and taught.
It must come to be tanned by the sun.
It must develop calluses by working.
   Its eyes are watery
   and its vision is distorted.
We must dry its eyes
   so that it can see clearly.
We have to work the fat off it
   to see if it can be a something.
It is ugly in its rebirth,
   but we don't know what it is yet.
It must use itself to see what it will be.
It leaves spots on the pavement.
It is big and unused.
It seems to have potential,
   just looking at it,
but until it does something,
   we will not know just how much.
A lot of effort must be expended,
   especially, at first.

ART

Whatever comes out,
when it comes out,
is meaningful
and has its place -
whether mundane, boring,
trite or uninteresting,
whether exciting, filled with insight,
philosophy, beauty or love.

It is also particular
upon the face of this earth
because it could not have been said,
or made or have come about
by another human
in the same way
or in the same year, month or day
or with the same words
or with the same overtones of feeling
or with the same connotations.

Therefore,
everything is valuable that comes out,
and is meaningful to someone
or something.
Even if it is nothing,
it is something.

Even if it is something to withhold
or something to shout about
or something to rework,
it has its place

and should be given its due,
and respected
and acknowledged
for what it is,
whatever it is.

For, it cannot be repeated,
even by the same individual,
and only comes out once
during a passing moment of time
and is entirely unique.

Therefore, whatever comes out
is an expression of male
or female,
and being human-made
and not nature-made,
is art.

Notes - Risking

Feeling dishonest and not liking ourselves for it, my new friend and I decided to confess the truth of our relationship to our respective families. We cared deeply about each other and felt that however unpleasant, we must address this new circumstance. The spouses and progeny reacted in accordance with their special characters and temperaments, but the consequence was the two husbands moved out of their houses and began alimony and child support payments. I lived in a cabin, baby-sat a house for a realtor and lived in a friend's guest quarters for the next year and a half.

In therapy I began revealing my hurts, examining past behavior leading to my present situation, relating former family episodes and doing the preparatory work necessary to finding the highly elusive *'self.'* I began a dream journal, wrote thoughts and feelings, and learned intellectually that feelings are *'self.'* I learned that dreams offer a direct view into the unconscious and drew pictures of emotionally charged situations and relationships. Outside of therapy, I told my new friend my concerns from the innocuous to the horrendous, and being a good listener and fascinated by the field of emotional health, she was of enormous help. I did the dot-dot-dot poems which leave the subject matter out, such as in *Over and Under,* and I began to *'claim my space'* as in *I Claim it Mine.* Until now I had always *reacted* to life. Now I was beginning to *act* on life. *Whistling* is an effort expressing who I felt was the real me; *Winnie* was not his own dog, nor had I been my own man.

In June of 1978, I discovered the portentous writings of the poet, Theodore Roethke who, in his book, *Words for the Wind*, frequently contrasted lines seemingly unrelated; *"How cool the grass is. / Has the bird left? / The stalk always sways. / Has the worm a shadow? / What do clouds say?"*

I thought I'd experiment with his method, *Moon Shattered*, being my first attempt. Carl Jung says, *"What is unconscious is projected."*

Writing *Roethke* poems, I found, is like automatic writing in poetic form. The lines are predisposed, like dreams, to come direct from the psyche. *The Heartsore* fell out on the page two poems later. Its subject is my unused, long buried, hard to look at, *'child within.'* The next day I justified him in *Art*. The Roethke method sent me like an arrow straight past poetry into a psychological forest.

Part 6 - Discovery

WHEN SHALL THE ... (Part 1)

When shall the . . .
And, in the morning, go . . .
And, then, shall that change anything?

And, when shall I . . .
For she said she would,
   but didn't.
And I am bitter
and shall not be contented,
for it is <u>my</u> life,
and <u>I'm</u> the one who pays.

Lost in the river of life.
   Through dark forests, I go,
   wondering about the light,
listening for rain
   and distant thunder,
   for rain shall save me.
   Lightly pattering on thick leaves,
   it comes, whispering, with the cool breeze.
Then, increasing in tempo,
   and soon is upon us
and we are the heart of the cloudburst
and our faces are drenched
   as we lift them
and we taste the cool rainwater
and our dry lips are soothed.
   The wrinkled brow eases
and a smile warms our faces,
having grown from the inside.
For peace is upon us

and we deserve it
for we have traveled far
and will not go that way again.
But, now is the time for reflecting,
and as the rain lessens,
so our contented, peaceful feelings
   turn to thoughtfulness
and we proceed, as before,
down the same trodden pathway,
hopeful and with renewed strength
   and new spirit
   and new step
and the forests change to meadows
   with wild flowers
   and crystal rivulets
   winding their unhurried way
   to the larger brooks
and we begin our exciting journey
   in earnest
   for we have a new bearing,
   a new essence,
   a new calling.
And it will enrich our lives
and we will grow
   and sing
   and draw
   and write
and make things we want to make.
   The most important being
   the making of ourselves,
for this shall be the richest work,
   the most rewarding work,
   the most meaningful
and fulfilling work we can do.

The journey could take us
   to the land of blue sky *(top)*
   and green grass *(bottom)*
and nothing else.

Just sky and grass,
   blue and green,
   clean and fresh
   invading our senses.
We could go to purple mountains
   against an orange sky
   with a red warlord sun
   about to set.
We may see silver clouds
   in fish forms
   gleaming in the airy heavens,
or one lone star, Venus,
   bright against the midnight blue
   of a tranquil sky.
Under the ground, could we go,
   through serpentine tunnels
   deep in the earth,
   where we find treasures
   rich beyond dreams;
   diamonds, emeralds
   friendships, loves
or, over the falls,
   falling free for miles,
   and entering cool, green water.
   Plunging deeply,
   through ever-greener,
   ever-darker colors and pressures
   with silver bubbles
   clustering about us

and suspended.
Then, effortlessly rising,
  plenty of breath,
  we enjoy our ascending.
Up from the dark green coolness
  rising with bubbles
to the silvery surface,
undulating, mirroring above,
and as we break through the surface
into raw sunlight,
  green trees,
  massive rocks and foliage
  and a fresh strong breeze,
we know that this is where we belong,
and everything feels right
  and connected,
and that we have achieved our final
  completeness.

Lifting from the water's surface,
  we might float
  like a bubble
  lightly born on the air
and drift out of the canyon,
  steep slopes descending,
over roads and pathways,
over the snake-like silvery river,
over the winding highways
  and traveling cars
  and clouds
  and sun,
immersed in the breeze and blue sky.
Over the villages, towns, cities
  of our birth,

we get the wide view,
the panorama of this green earth
from which we have been born.

We understand
    by our under-view
    and our overview
that this is truly where we live.
That no one can take it from us.

And that it is good.
We welcome it
    for it is beautiful
and we see it from the overview
    and the under-view
and we claim it ours
and it claims us for its own
and we are inseparable,
    its follies, our follies,
    its joys, our joys,
for it is
and we are
and we are it
and it is us
and to hurt a part of it
    is to hurt each of us
and to love it,
is to be loved by it.

And we must not forget the intimate things.
    The beetles, hurriedly
    crossing the pathways.
Spring green grass shoots.
Bees, struggling

to find a way out
through a partially closed window,
not seeing the opening.
The silent worm, content in its bed of warm earth,
   and our intimate daily relations,
   our lovingness,
   our angriness,
   our unfulfilledness,
   our hopefulness,
and the knowledge that,
   though we are all together,
yet each is alone.

That we can never know, fully,
what another feels,
for there are no rules,
   and there is no right or wrong,
   only ebbing and flowing.
I give way to your push,
you yield to my advance.
And this is the way
toward true satisfaction
   and fulfillment
   and happiness
   in this rich time of our life.

For when two yield or push at the same time,
   there is no motion.
But, the ebb and the flow,
   the pushing and yielding,
this makes for motion
   and excitement
   and getting things done
   in a loving and expressive way.

For by yielding,
    we acknowledge the other
    in his or her pushing,
and in sensing the other's yield,
    we are aware of our own
    unmistakable affect.
And, so, to ebb and flow,
    this is the way to go.

WHAT SHE SAID - (Part 1)

7/78

She said to me ...
and the buried light appeared;
    came swinging in the attic
    of lost memory
and illumined, brilliant,
that one lost instant,
when, transformed
    from boy to ghost,
    I saw that tortured face.
It came, the light, on a sweltering hand
    and showed me the way.
Shall I have the courage to see?
Can I gaze on that lost face?
Those wrinkled lines around the eyes?
    That wistful smile
    that held me close?
Those eyes that claimed me,
    "Mine, for all my time!?"
For, she would never let me down,
    but would rather lose her life.
    I loved her, so,

with golden rays of light
   gleaming from my eyes
   as she held me close.

And then the picture darkened,
   faded from my view,
   by one last remark,
   one last glance,
by some last gesture,
   taken heavily.
   It came. My loss.

Or was it insidious?
Did it creep and steal upon my back
   from the darkness
   of my time with her,
   after . . . ?
Until, without warning,
I knew the door had closed,
   never to be reopened.
Perhaps, now,
   "like sight, once lost,
   regained for just an instant,
   and then forever gone,"
   I hope.
I loved her so,
   and she, me,
and would read me stories
   and I would journey with her
   through many a golden land
   of love.
   And we were one,
   and basked in each other's aura
   and strode down golden trails

strewn with poetry
and adventure.

I loved her so,
  and she, me.
Until the specter appeared!
  In what strange shape?
  Was it my blond-haired brother
  with innocent eyes
  and lashes, long and dark,
that beguiled my dear one away?
Was it he that diverted our way of being?

Sent me on the course
  of slithering monsters
  with swollen eyes?
Was it he that sent me adrift,
  unknowingly, a fool on the high seas?
Was it he that sent me stupidly on my way
  to bumble in doorsteps
  to beg for a pittance
  to thank the whip for the lash,
  or fitfully doze
  these forty years.

Probably not.
  I'll never know.

WHAT SHE SAID - (Part 2)

7/78

Dim, the lights in dark doorways.
Silently the rat rustles the scraps.

I love the golden eyes of eagles.
Clouds drift and dream of rain and sun.
   Little does the . . .
   in the heart of the . . .
   know that . . .

What a surprise
   Her white thighs.
She told me I shouldn't
   and lowered her eyes.
Her footfall came with the wind.
He reached for the knob on the door.

I loved her thighs
   as I loved the moon.
We know . . .
   but we don't . . .
But we can . . .
   I love you, lizard.
Beetles strike out with decision.
   Tools are built with precision,
and so is mine.

BLUE, THE GRASS
OF THE HAPPIER HEART

Blue is the grass of
   the happier heart,
but shall not grow
where charred trunks
stab a hopeless sky
and the black-sand desert reaches

and pavement lines converge.
There, rocks pray
to superheated air
and die inside.
There, the sun hangs limp
and shall not be revived.
There, just my heart
and a tiny fish,
    content in its bowl,
have lived and loved,
    survived.

ALIVE, HE GOES, INTO THE COFFIN

7/78

He sold her down the river.
   I loved to touch her cunt.
She used to snuggle close
   but doesn't anymore.
I loved her thigh above her stocking.
Her tongue struck lightning to my cock.
   I loved to love her love.
Eager was the hasty heart.
   She shimmied on the floor.
The eyes of friends were lusting.
   My bleeding heart was sore.
   She took me up the ladder,
   led me by the nose,
   and let me put my burning hand
   above her silky hose.
I sold her down the river.
   There's anguish in my heart.
My fat and watery eyesore crying evermore.

What did I do to give her away
in those early days of my lost love?
Her heart was bright
   and her love was true.
She wrote me letters.
   I wrote, too.
The boys at the party lapped her up.
I lay bleeding on the stair,
my fat and watery eyesore
   exposed for all to see.
I dammed my feelings,
   corked them tight,
decided to break my little boy.
I put him, screaming, alive,
   into the coffin
and swallowed my soul.

THE FOREST HOLDS THE ANSWER

7/78

Marriage is a fake.
Trees, still, on the prairie.
She bundled up her skirt.
   I wait and waiting, wait.
She locked the door and locked her cunt.
   Refrigerators never close.
This car needs gas.
   Oranges are ripe after seven.
The bedclothes tell a tale.
   Two bright shoes.
I love her walking pattern.
"April is in My Mistress' Face,"
   but in her heart, a cold September.
They both were fishmongers.

I eat my peach, then toss the pit.
    Summer spells trouble.
The tug of the silken cord.
    To cut my cord
    is to cut my life.
Lying adrift, he goes with the tide.
    Anguish strikes his face.
He whispers to God
    who does not hear,
so empty is his space.
    When will the silk cord break?
I see him drifting out to sea,
    returning to some lost friend.
He shall live his life
    and shall not sell another down the river.
Come to grips with a roving bear.
    She lighted thirteen candles.
The smoke of the fire eternally present.
    I leapt and leaping free . . .
Put the candle on the table.
    Can't we have a party,
    you and me?
I see her waist, her hips, her dress,
    seducing every eye.
I love to see them flowing,
    but also want to cry.
When will the . . .
    In the time of the . . .
    have the power to . . .
    and will be full.
I live for the glutted state.
    Where will I go
    if I'm not with me?
The forest holds the answer.
    So does the sea.

RAIN, WHERE ARE YOU?

Rain, where are you?
I need you, now.
I need to feel your cool breeze
    blowing up from the west.
I need to feel the dampness
    in your air.
I need to see you light
    the warm night sky
and hear your approaching
    rumblings.
When will you come?

LOVED LAND

Summer weeds delight the eye.
The elm tree sways and purrs.
Cherry blossoms sing in sweet surrender.

I dig the digging clay.
I climb the singing tree.
I bloom, my heart, as the orchard.

Sun and wind, thick, like snow.
Quietly I sit between
    and watch the panoramic games;
"heat lightning."
Thunder rolls in rhythmic wonder.
Lightly rest my eyelids
    in the middle of the rain.

Moon and stars, mirror
   in the magic mind.
I bask in the love of a sweetened heart
   and eat the peach of contented time.

GORILLA DREAM

8/78

Yellow was the hasty heart.
I loved her in the morning
when the dew was on the ground.
I remember mamma in the spring.
How does this thing figure?
The yellow rose has no hose.
Theoretically, time will tell.
Hello, dolly, what's in it for you?
Along came a blackbird
and snipped off her nose.
Fourteen hundred elephants
trampled down the grass.
A truly devastating region.
All clear on the western front.
"I'm free," cried Sally.
Easter eggs make lots of sense.
I want a banana for my very own.
She peeled me a grape.
Daddy was a rouser.
Simple Simon met a Pieman.
'April is in my mistress' face.
But in her heart, a cold September.
I want Mamma, but she doesn't want me.

SHOWER DREAM

8/78

Now, in the dawn of the new day.
April is gone from my mistress' face.
And in her heart is nothing.
I have come to the vantage point.
Silence is in my body.
Where have you gone, sweet birds?
I love life with a twist.
"Isn't that so?" said the crow.
Hallelujah! I'm a bum.
Snow falls in South Nantucket.
When will the . . . ?
Ice is on the window pane.
Hello, dolly, what's your story?
See the animal twist and writhe.
How are little toys made?
I remember Mamma in the spring.
Aftershocks are shocking.
His brain whirled
   like an egg beater in Hades.
See here, mister! I love, too!
The Jack-in-the-Box knows.
He loved his fingers and toes.
Life is lonely as it goes.
Where does Harriet figure in all this?
Fourteen hundred elephants
   tiptoe on the grass.
Let me have that fly swatter.
I can take care of myself.
But what about all these people?
Serrania loves the dog.
The dog is in the kitchen.

So is the cat.
Hello, dolly, what's your name?
Give me some skin, pal.
I know you,
But you don't know me.
Time will wear an even rug.
Simple Simon met a Pieman
   going to the fair.
Said Simple Simon
to the Pieman,
   "Let me taste your ware."
The idyllic flower bloomed.
Hello, Guy, what's your story?
The Goodyear Blimp floats high.
Sometimes I think of Mamma.
Now is the time for sun.
Give me some skin.
Sometimes the burner is high.
Swing high, swing low,
   sweet chariot.
   Comin' for to carry me home.
(Rest of Song)

THE BURNING TREE

8/78

I would the burning tree
ask its question.
For, in the evening,
starlight whispers, softly.
Calls to me in pussy willow tones
that reach my middle mind
and blow cool zephyrs

across the shallows of my heart.
I know you, mind.
And you, feather-softened thoughts
that yield not, but as the stone,
press their burning way.

Come to me sweet one.
You, with smiling eye.
Linger softly in my soul
and cover me with lemon-love.
for, I do.

Notes - Discovery

The accent in the preceding works is clearly psychological and not so much poetic. Experimenting with *Roethke* poems was more like doing automatic writing up and down rather than across the page. I stopped thinking of myself as a poet and began searching in earnest for something that was desperate. As dream journals became the higher priority, some of that material drifted into *Roethke* writing and I quickly saw the connection between dreams and poetry: both came from the right brain, center of feelings, instincts, urges and non-verbal resolutions. I avoided editing my work to better examine the sequential purity and unconscious material so blatantly exposing itself. I heard about and tried left-hand writing. The left hand, being controlled by the right brain, would give me information directly from *'the one who knows.'* I found this method of inner access a powerful tool, able to uncover what I considered important insights on the road to *'self,'* especially when put into context with counseling and dream work. Developing methods, I was on the move.

In *What She Said,* I look for the time of my original *split* from *myself, . . . when transformed from boy to ghost . . ."* In *Blue the Grass of the Happier Heart,* the tiny fish is my survivor-self. *Alive He Goes Into the Coffin,* expresses my inadequate, jealous-of-mother/wife self. *Rain* questions when my ordeal will end. The collection of apparently unrelated lines in *The Forest Holds the Answer, He Put Me on the Hose, Gorilla Dream,* and *Shower Dream* are what I began calling, *psycho-poems.*

Existing now as a record of personal transition, they came about thusly: I would dream a very graphic, memorable dream and write it down immediately. Staying in the mood of the dream, I'd write successive lines on a sheet giving each a number and following two rules;

(1)   Look deeply for honest meaning.
(2)   Trust the first thing entering my mind and write it down quickly.

When this was completed, I'd set forth highlights of my dream in lines 1, 2, 3, etc. as I had in writing psycho-poems and interpret it similarly.

WRITING DOWN SHOWER DREAM

I am in bed with someone I can't see, but suspect is a man considerably older. I think he is related to me and I have no animosity toward him. I am also in bed with a beautiful, buxom woman who is young and delectable. I felt that sometime before she has made love to the other male in bed. I think I would like to, too, and so cuddle close to her and hug her and kiss her neck and face. She is unresponsive. I am disappointed and feel rejected. She does not indicate we will ever make love. She gets up and puts on her clothes to go somewhere. I get up, too, and decide to take a shower.

The strange shower setup is located in an adjacent patio next to the bedroom. There are plants, a roof and shelves. I turn on the water that comes out of a much too low spout that appears made from a rusty can with holes. Getting under the shower, I discover I still have on my now damp shirt and other clothes. I remove them, fold them and put them aside on the dresser. The shower water splatters on them anyway.

I discover I have on another shirt and take that one off only to find I have on yet another, which I also remove. I put them on a shelf and in a drawer. As I open the drawer, a spray from the shower again goes in the drawer to wet the clothes. I take off another shirt, getting it wet as I get under the shower. I finally do get all the shirts off and discover I am wearing jockey shorts and must take them off, too. I'm amazed at how many clothes I have to take off to get a simple shower.

Retaining the mood of the dream, I'd write numbered lines successively down the page as they occurred to me. I'd write at least 20, or until finished.

NUMBERING DREAM LINES
and
INTUITIVE INTERPRETATION IN ITALICS

1   **Now, in the dawn of a new day,**
    Now when I finally have some insight.

2   **April is gone from my mistress' face.**
    The hurt look of my mother is not so much.

3   **And in her heart is nothing.**
    Of course she knew nothing of my plight.

4   **I have come to the vantage point.**
    I have finally seen some truths.

5   **Silence is in my body.**
    And I feel quieted.

6   **Where have you gone sweet birds?**
    The hurt look and anxiousness has evaporated.

7   **I love life with a twist.**
    I love life, but the consequences of my unnatural

mother-bond due to early trauma at a key transition
time proved troublesome.

8   **Isn't that so, said the crow?**
Mother would agree with me.

9   **Hallelujah, I'm a bum!**
Hooray! I've discovered my genuine self!

10 **Snow falls in South Nantucket.**
I never thought this would happen.

11 **When will the … ?**
But I wonder when it all take effect and my personality
and attitude will show significant changes.

12 **Ice is on the windowpane.**
There are still things to overcome.

13 **Hello, Dolly, what's your story?**
I wonder what I will be like with this new insight?

14 **See the animal twist and rise.**
Certainly I'm in a period of rapid changes.

15 **How are little toys made?**
I wonder how insights affect change.

16 **I remember Mama in the spring.**
I remember Mom long ago when Dave was born.

17 **Aftershocks are shocking.**
Dave's birth was a shock I didn't expect.

18 **His brain whirled like an egg beater in Hades.**
To my four-year-old self, Dave's birth was
mind-boggling.

19 **See here, mister! I love, too!**
I wanted to tell mother and dad, but I was too young
and couldn't.

20 The Jack-in-the-Box knows.

That which was hidden came out suddenly.

21 Etcetera.

The results were astonishing in their accuracy and provided me an all but infallible means to reach non-verbal, feeling information long hidden from the unconscious. The rules being:

A **Have the dream and write it down.**

B **Do a *not-too-intellectual* psycho-poem.**

C **Number the lines.**

D **Interpret the *"nonsense"* from life experience.**

E **<u>Set down</u> the *highlights* of the interpretation.**

Sample of highlights*:*

    1 I wish to hug and kiss a beautiful woman who has just made love to an older person *(dad)* I also love.

    2 I do not succeed, though when I hug her she feels warm and comforting.

    3 Nevertheless, I feel rejected. If she makes love to him, why not me?

    4 The shower continues to wet the many clothes I take off.

    5 Am astounded how many clothes I have to take off before getting a simple shower.

F *<u>Interpret</u>* the highlights:

FINAL ANALYSIS

Mother and dad love each other very much, and I love dad but want mother in the same way I see him as having her.

Though I don't receive the same favors as dad, mother is nice to be near and I long for her exclusively.

I feel rejection and enter a questioning and confused state.

I find myself in this state for a long period of time until, finally, to ease the pain, begin peeling off layers of myself, adding insight to insight to reveal the necessary truth.

I am astounded at how many insights are required to finally get naked, that is, to reveal my natural self.

In this way I will be able to write a simple analysis such as that for the Shower Dream Psycho-poem:

Note: Dreams are usually attempts by the organism to resolve or assimilate events that have recently happened that have not been thoroughly considered, evaluated or absorbed. Some events can also trigger old material that has not been adequately considered, evaluated or absorbed in one's own past. Therefore, dreams can be of varying length, and interpretations will take longer or shorter, but in each case it can be an adventure that is always worth discovering and revealing. What is learned can never be un-learned; therefore, progress is continually made. In my case, with a year or so of work, it eventually led to an epiphany, the cornerstone information leading to a change in attitude and life.

Part 7 - Processing

SHADOW DANCE

Now the shadows
begin their dance
on walls of silence.
And flowers bloom
where once the driven sand
lay barren.

I know the heart
in all its beating,
and blood, well driven,
sounding on the temple's shores.

Little did the cavern
know of morning light.
Little did the seed
anticipate the rain.

I see you, little boy.
Smile in the face
of tears long shed.
Hit me little one,
I deserve your blow.
Hit me, hit me.
I love you so.

WHERE SHALL YOU GO?

Where shall you go,
sweet hopes for a loving life?

Where shall life take you, now?
Into the world to work your way?
     To this attraction, then that?
And finally resolve on some special one?
And what about me?
Shall I die a thousand deaths?
Shall I mourn through my last hour?
Shall you be some spent pit
aching in my heart?
I suspect you will.
(I lament that which cannot be resolved.)
Where shall you go?
Where shall I go,
now that we are truly

finished?

THE YOUNG MAN'S FANCY

4/79

For in the evening,
the young man's fancy
does turn to thoughts of love.
And this young butterfly
shall be denied no more.
Nor shall the willow,
springing from the river bottom.
I know you, soul.
You want red meat
and green things to eat.

Dead men speak no more.
The stone sits, heavy,

on the desert floor.

Without growth,
only death remains.
Be near, sweet spirit.
I breathe your fragrance.
I hold you to me
    like a mother does, her baby.
I clasp you to my breast,
    like a brother home from war.
I am not lonely,
    nor shall I be, again.
I have you, my soul,
for my friend.

WORK TO DO

4/79

It is I who am here.
There, are you.
Thank me, fine friend,
    for the distinction.
Kill that tomato.
Up from the darkness
    of whole existence,
    she waddled toward the toilet.
I heard her scream when she landed.
There was no time for blackberry pie.
I wanted to listen,
    but she would not share.
I set the trap, then ran for my life.
My face was gaunt,
    but my arms were full.

She wouldn't listen,
    so I shouted,
"Come here, baby,
    or we're through!"
I heard the sobbing in the night.
    It carried for miles.
"What do you mean, duty?"
I lifted the lid and looked, then,
    into the maelstrom I leapt with a fury.
"I don't know why I keep wishing this way."
Come along, black cat,
    we have work to do.

FACE OF GOD

4/79

    Why are you trapped behind those bars, my friend?
I trapped myself.
    A novel idea. But, to what gain?
This way, I do not have to see the face of God.
    I see. And is that so bad, the face of God?
I don't know, I have never seen him.
    Look, then!
Are you God!?
    No.
I don't know where to look.
    Why don't you want to see the face of God?
I am afraid He will demand something of me.
    And, if he does?
I shall not be able to give it.
    Why not?
He wants my only heart.
    And can you not open it to him?

No.

   Why not?

I have closed it, forever.

   Why so?

If I open it, I shall see the face of Death.

   And is that so bad, the face of Death?

Yes.

   You are afraid to see the face of God because he
may require you to open your heart, and if you do,
you shall see the face of Death!

Yes.

   You stand here, then, afraid of God and Death.

Yes.

   A limbo state.

Yes.

   Afraid of God and Death.

Yes.

WHO SHALL BE THE WISER

4/79

I must inhale
the thick perfumes
of the wild, love flower.
Come with me, lusty one,
be my pregnant queen.
Let us meld,
creamy, into the day
and permeate the soil.

The third eye kept smiling.
I listened to the wind.
The day was ripped with sunshine.

I tasted chocolate peanuts.
Ed was sure I was right.
I see a vortex in the sky,
the baby a lonely dot
sucked away by the wind.

The dull-eyed stare
of the contented cow
is not the breaking wave.
I'll not have my neck broke, twice.
Tearfully, in tones precise,
across the blackened meadow,
she called to me,
"I'll never come again."

Once, hot oatmeal
across the Canadian lake,
stifled the call of the loon.
But, oranges hang high
on dead-wood trees
and blue jays appear
in the strangest places.
Lie with me, naked lady.
In full sun.
Who shall be the wiser?

THE SPOTTED SNAKE

5/79

On the garden path,
coiled the spotted snake.
She peacefully glistened.
and whispered love

in honeyed tones
to the gentle mouse,
whose eyes, black with wonder,
    listened.
The yellow, spotted snake,
whose sultry skin,
harmoniously mixed
with shades of brown and gray,
    spoke of love
and life together,
her reasons tight,
like bricks in a wall.
The mouse, intrigued,
could not deny the logic
of this would-be mate
nor a quiet sense of death.

MORE ANGUISH

5/79

I have anguish
in my heart.
Someone I cared for,
care for,
is with me,
no more.
I miss her touch,
her eyes, her kiss.
I miss her loving attention,
her delicate beauty,
the sweetness of her taste.
I wish she were with me,
and now, and yet,

the ugly reservation
rudely appears
destroying the dream,
her dream, my dream,
exploding the love
in my heart.

MIDNIGHT THOUGHTS

7/79

And now again
the earth is without form
and void and blackness
is upon the face of the deep.
Tired, vulnerable,
I sit on the edge of tears
afraid of night's blackness.
An internal grieving
sucks me away.
I would that I'd blow away,
the way the wind blows,
as a leaf, swiftly,
over the hill,
and the wind in its whistling,
as it whips the sky,
leaves white streaks.
I see the mountains
rise against the sun.
Immense, our planet,
great in its turning.
Pinpoints of light
penetrate the blackness,
itchy like prickles,

sour like pickles.
A lion roars,
and on the continent,
terror fills the heart
of fleshy, animate food.
Nonsense is
as nonsense does.
I like potatoes
when they're mashed up tight.
Sing me a song
   before I sleep.
I love peaches
in the mourning,
   but sometimes the night,
and a little pot of tea,
   infiltrates my room,
and a piece of toast will do,
   penetrates my flesh,
to begin a sunny day,
   assuring my doom.
My heartbeat
will drive it out
and replace the cold terror
with warm flesh
content in the afternoon.
And the evening sleeps,
having been sung to
by frogs and crickets
and creeping things.
I do love daisies
blowing in the wind.
   Listen to me, mamma,
   hear how I cry,
   sing me a song, too,

so I won't die.
I have a little yellow wagon
that follows me around
in which I keep my things.
Hello, loved one.
Have you had me to eat?
I hunger for you as well.
Please eat me with kissable lips.
Ply me with love *'til I bloom.'*
I'll speak quietly from my heart.
You'll listen quietly with your heart.
We shall speak
as we stand close
and have nothing to say.
Breast to breast,
heart to heart,
soul to soul,
we speak,
we know,
we love.
     "I'm getting married in the morning!"
The essence of life
is living.
The essence of happiness
is being.
     "Ding, dong, the bells are going to chime!"
I want a watermelon
and I want to spit the seeds
See the grass grow.
See the tree wave.
See the bush flow,
in the heat, rising.
I see trees
shaking their leaves.

I see roots
reaching into soil.
Sing me some sweet song,
you with love to spare,
that I may sleep
and sleeping, come together.
It is time you and I became good friends;
walked in the garden
of friendly love,
spoke as brothers speak,
strong, willful, loving,
stout of limb,
stout of heart,
stout of intent.
Listen to the *little* voices.
Sometimes I'd have an amplifier
that I could hear them better.
　The essence of drawing
　is to get it right.
To say what is meant.
To do what must be done
as the plant does what must be done
to produce its flower.
The essence of growth
is growing.
The essence of song is singing.
The essence of heart
is its beating.
The essence of process,
is proceeding.
　"Roll out the barrel . . ."
A wine is rich
if aged in wood
and drunk in the right frame of mind.

And so is milk.
And I am a brick,
strong, static,
compressive, tight.
I sit on the ground
and I like it here.
I am a stick,
flexible, light.
I bend when I want
and will not break.
I am a flag.
I fly on a pole.
And when I am flying,
I'm living.
Give me a penny
and I'll give you a dime.
For such is my gladness
and so rich is my heart.
Give me your bike
and I'll give you my home,
for so do I like you,
    rich as you are.
Give me your smile
and I'll give you my heart,
for ready it is,
enthusiastic, strong.
I love you,
tree, waving.
Blow me a kiss.
I love you, tall grass,
warm in the field.
I love you strong rain
striking my mouth.
I love you weariness.

Time for your sleep.
Contented, you sleep.
Goodnight.

A LOVE POEM

11/79

I should have moved
into her space.
　I should have encroached, sweetly,
into the place of her cheek and mouth.
I should have felt her hair
　against my cheek
and breathed her being.
I should have lightly
　grazed her chin
with my lips,
　　eyes, half closed.
I should have seen her lashes
　drop quickly down,
and looked in her eyes,
　deeply,
and smoothed her hair
from her cheek,
　shadows darkening.
I should have told her,
　wordless,
with my presence.

Notes- Processing

*T*hough I had reached an important insight resulting in the almost total release of long standing hypertension based on anxiety, I felt my work incomplete. During 1979 I continued to concentrate on the emotional content and meaning of dreams which I discovered were a more effective tool for self-discovery. However, I made a few poetic attempts indicative of my emotional flow.

Self-congruency is anticipated in *Shadow Dance.* Though my *'inner child'* and I were still strangers, I had at least confirmed his existence and becoming conversant was my next task. I nurtured our connection by listening carefully for the faint almost inaudible messages emanating from that cavity somewhere between navel and neck. Encouraged by my friend, I began trusting this *'little voice'* as actually the long sought *'self'*; that vulnerable part of me so heavily defended for so many years. I turned up the receiver to better hear the subtle convictions from the defended prisoner below. How easily the injured *'self'* grows its protective shell. How impenetrable that defensive barrier. How difficult the frightening work to break through it, and then find *The Heartsore,* unused, un-nurtured, the neglected and sometimes hated Child King imprisoned within his castle. If feelings are *'self,'* I reasoned, then, if I trust my feelings, I'll trust my *'self.'* I'll trust myself! I'll be self-trusting! If trust and love are inseparable, then I'll be self-loving. If I have self-love/trust then I have self-esteem! If I have self-esteem, I have the capability for joy! It seems so easy, but it's not, but it's not hopeless.

In *Where Shall You Go?*, *The Spotted Snake* and *More Anguish,* I continued to test my decision to leave my wife, to realize the hopelessness of reconciliation and to lament our unfulfilled dreams. A processing conglomerate of grief over loss of my dream, despair over my ill-fated mother-bond, loving another, finding self and final joyfulness is expressed in the hopeful *Midnight Thoughts.*

Having strong feelings for my new friend, I was able to compare them with those for my former mate. What should have been happening all along in my marriage, but wasn't is expressed in *A Love Poem.* It was clear I was on my correct path. I'd continue the divorce, trust my new found *'self'* and begin to accept what appeared to be my new destiny.

Part 8 - Acceptance

WINTER RAINS

I love winter rains
as I do cold winds
that whisper
in the hollows of my bones.

They sing,
those slippery hollows,
of immortal life
as well as death.

I love wintry fog
that settles, restless,
on the night
and then advances,
stiff and formal,
through my face.

I love brittle stars,
those of Orion's belt,
Venus and Mars;
they float on mist
and winter rains
run, coolly,
in the hollows of my face.

And, I love
stars and fog,
cold winds and rain,
and death,
as well as life.

FROM THE TEEMING CENTER OF THE AGITATED MIND

2/80

From the teeming center of the agitated mind, she grew with a boundless power and a mindless speed.

Spilling life's blood into the turmoil of oblivion, crying from the inside of a soul turned black, she screamed her presence to the impartial night.

The hungry jackals lowered their yellow eyes and resumed duties to their prey.

I prefer the sunny optimism of an ignorant daisy to the silent terrors of an ingrown mind, don't you?

Check which you prefer:
   ___the sated stillness of an emancipated cow, or
   ___the poverty of hollow bones on broken rocks?

She greeted me with full stomach resting against her lungs and said she'd overheard the stifled crying of the baby in the loft as the sawdust sifted, softly, in the stillness of the gloom.

When I looked up, I saw black cats with yellow eyes leap through brittle-starred, black heavens, teeth bared, in an anticipatory grin; which made me quizzical;

I don't know why miniscule insects climb lofty anise plants; but, then, neither does the shrimp boat gliding above its shadow. I feel sure another yesterday will be on us by tomorrow,

and when yesterday is now,
can tomorrow be far behind?

I feel sure that it can't be, don't you?

HE LEAPS

3/80

On the breakfast table
the young, fat cat,
eyes on the counter,
concentrates on his leap.

He leaps!

Paws outstretched,
eyes intent,
body tense.

He misses!
Tangled on the floor.

How surprising.
How discouraging.
How humiliating.
Especially, for a cat.
Until I remember;

He did leap.

THE VOICE IN THE MIST

3/80

I don't know how long she had
been whispering to me in the dark.
But the clock's yellow hand
pointed suddenly to seven
and struck three times.

For the fifth time
I turned again
and settled into my dream.

White mist moves, cold,
along solemn shores
of a soft wave sea.

"When will you be back?"
(I resume my conversation.)

And the lonely voice,
lost in the mist
that lingers in hollows
of the soft wave sea,
replied to me.

"When the clock strikes seven."
"But, the hand points to three!"
(Anxiously, I cry.)

"What is your problem?"
The phrase drifts in the air
then blends with the mist.

"But, I don't understand."
(I lay on my back
on the cold, wet sand.)

"You will," said the voice,
"when the red moon lifts
from the tense, black sea."

Perspiring, I wake.
The clock's yellow hand
points to seven
and strikes seven.

I pull back blankets
and worry myself to work.

CONTENT, FREE, FALLING

3/80

I visualize myself
plunged into the darkness
of obliviousness and rain.

The wind howls from the north.
Living things are silent.
Streams of crystal water
prostrate behind the gale,
peel away from pointed ends
of twigs and leaves.

There is no opening
in the black clouds.
Sleet from the fury
of the chaotic winds
stings my face and hands.

Yet, I proceed
with joyous heart,
warm in my clothes
and free.

Let the wind howl and whine.
Let the rain bluster its way
through the long night.
I don't give a damn!
I'm free!
I'll follow my heart,
   my trail,
   my purpose or bent,
   my whim or joy
and the devil be damned!

I'll walk to the edge of the land
   where the wind trails off
   and the rain streams over
   and the black night sky
   opens below, as well as above,
   and button my jacket
   and leap.

I'll fall and falling, fall,
   feel safe.
Secure in the warmth
of my body and spirit.

I'll fall through perpetual darkness
   at home in a contented heart.

Falling, free, falling
   through the night rain,
   the sleet, the wind, the space.
That yawning, black, open space.

   That immense womb
   of the eternal living.

Contentedly I fall, sure,
　　warm in my clothes.
Though storms howl about me
　　and sleet stings my face.
　　Yet, I am smiling,
　　certain and content
in the warmth of my body heat,
　　and invincible heart.
At peace in my clothes.
Falling through sleet
　　and blackness
　　and rain.

YOUR NATURAL RIGHT

3/80

Beneath the black sea
of the abysmal mind,

lurking in the stagnant soup
of *"can't"* and being victim,

occupying space within
the thickness of, *"if only,"*

lives a dragon pure as sky.
Dragon, feel your strength.

Inhale the terrifying
richness of your soul.

Let loose that roar of devastation
and let us see your leaping flame

and feel your power of destruction.
Claim your space
like the conquering sun
and show death and darkness
whom it is they fear.

Blister your inertia.
Fry your way to truth.
Burn your way to freshness
and to freedom
and to light;

your natural right.

THE CROW

3/80

The crow on the fence post
    sits, convinced.
She flaps and stretches
    and assumes a pose
of tense repose.
    The sun is hot.
The crow, more so,
    because of her blackness.
Her yellow eyes
    burrow deep.
Her expression, mean,
    behind her beak,
    unrelenting.
I wonder when she'll fly away.
She stays, it seems,
    for hours,

watching, waiting,
cocking her head,
   burrowing her mean eyes,
staring, searching,
   observing.
Nothing escapes her.
What she doesn't see
with her eyes
she feels through the quills
   of her feathers.

Her essence is everywhere.
She permeates
   the atmosphere.
She stands, the center
   of her own aura
   of sensitivity
and meanness,
   and I, the object,
   must *"cotton up"*
   or receive the big,
   "Or else!"
She sees in me
   something vile
I see not in myself.
She does not see
   how beautiful I am.

LOVE

3/80

Now the angels
   from the darkened room

begin their incantations.

Like an expanding plant,
    with startling speed,
    fills the room.

The hand of mind
    extends
to clasp a welcome soul,

and peace descends,
    a golden joy,
like honey on an almond bun,
as love,
    that solid heart,
lifts her hem
    and takes the throne.

MORE "ONE"

3/80

Being *"one with the universe"*
    does not mean

I am a small part of a large universe.
    it means

I __am__ the universe.

BECOMING WHOLE

3/80

Now that the intrepid adventurer
   has dimmed the light
   of youthful ardor
and has begun his advancing
   in crazy swirls,
limp like a hand,
   solid like a fist,
and the moons of Orion
   are spilling their silvery light,
slow motion, into the emptiness
   to bathe the eyes of wonder,
   stimulate the mind
   and wake the dormant heart,
I feel those gentle hands
   with billowing sleeves
lifting my feelings
   of reality
   and peace
   and love
into the strong light
   of truth
as I become whole.

SONG OF THE PASSERBY

3/80

The silver streaks
   of graying hair
fell gently to her shoulder,
and on the steps

of City Hall
the wind was getting colder.

The wintry winds descending
   blew cobwebs from her mind
   and *"wisdom"* took its rightful place
   but not the proper kind.

Chorus:
   So, I say,
   "Bullshit, bullshit.
   Won't you be my bullshit friend?
   Bullshit, bullshit,
   bullshit, shit on you."
So, I say,
   "Bullshit, bullsh . . ."
(Trails off in distance.)

MAGIC STONE

3/80

I have a magic stone
   through which I see
   the order of my life.

It is beautiful and rare
   like a moonstone,
   opalescent,
   textured
and just the proper weight.

It has organic
surface patterns,

designs
and arrangements,
both irregular and smooth.
It is the stone
of my life.

When I look intensely
into it,
the translucent stone
like deep water,
becomes crystal clear.
It magnifies anything
at which I choose
to look.
It brings whatever I desire
into crystal clarity,
optically correct
and pure.
Pock-marked, pitted
upon first seeing,
my stone,
yet, when I look intensely into it,

I see all I wish to behold,
magnified and clear.

SHOWTIME

3/80

At nighttime
I sit, my back
against a stone wall in the patio.
I hold a tall poplar branch

high in the air
extending above the wall.
A real poplar branch
from a strong, live tree
within the patio
waves, blows, comes and goes.
I wave my branch, too,
in harmony with the living branch,
so that others,
when they see the branches waving
from beyond the wall,
will think my branch
springs from a living tree,
coming and going,
waving and blowing.
I cannot perfectly
imitate the real tree,
but, I do put on
a reasonable show.

THUS, IT WILL EVER BE

4/80

My memory returns,
jogged off center
by the strong winds
blistering
between the canyon walls,
clean and crisp.
Razor edges of black shadows
cut the mind
in tan and black
leaving the *"three's a pageant,"*

Mars, Jupiter, Saturn
in their precisely
changing relationships
to freeze in the blackness
of outer space,
shimmering their messages
to waiting eyes
and minds,
calling to the souls of man,
the species.
From the inception
they've danced the answer,
yet, we do not perceive it,
not having the proper sensors,
but only minds
and beautiful bodies.
We sit,
ignorant bumpkins,
and dangle our legs
over the black chasm
and ask our silly questions
and the celestial pageant answers,
and we do not understand,
and so, we ask again,
and the answer's
in the very air.
Yet, we hear or see it not,
but continue to ask,
and so on,
and so on,
generation upon generation,
and I suspect,
thus, it well ever be.

NOTES FROM THE UNCONSCIOUS

4/80

Why not
　　the intrepid daisy?
For who can taste
　　its journey to the dying sky?
I'd like to
　　whistle up some pig meat myself,
　　little darling,
　　at least enough
to last us *'til we're home,*
　　content, in bed'.
The zoo is the place for you,
　　silly one.
Can't you make your silly way
　　through this vast garden?
Here, don't you like this
　　yellow rose,
or this bright daffodil?
Reminds you of yourself,
　　does it?
Well! No wonder,
　　the way you've been eating
　　these soggy days.
It's a wonder
　　you've not got
　　jock rot
　　of the cerebellum.
Well, give it time,
　　give it time.
You'll know what to do
　　when you're
　　just a little older.

Of course, the great horse trader
   in the sky
may be after you by then
   with his divine lasso.
But, who is the wiser?
I don't whistle Dixie
   to everyone,
especially
   when I'm sober.

GOOD "OLD" DAYS

4/80

Hey, there,
   simple minded soul!
   What have you got to chew on?
   Do you like your life?
   Or is it a pain
   in the you-know-what?
Maybe the golden goose
   will give you his egg.
But then,
   might as well
hope to walk on water.
I know a magic jackass,
   but he's too stubborn to move.
   I'm tired of waiting.
Maybe the stars
   will become confused,
forget which way to turn,
   zag then zig,
this way, that way,
   in swooping patterns

bumping into each other
   in some mad night display.
Will that answer
   your crazy question?
Or the clouds may become
   a solid chunk
   and fall, plunk,
   on the ground.
Or the rocks
   float away
like the red balloon
   from the picture
   of the same name.
Or the sun
   flare bright blue
   and go out,
leaving its after-image,
   dissolving
on your retina.
I know little tricks
with which to trick
   the mind.
   Tricky Dick,
   they'd call me,
in them days
of common nonsense.
Them days when we'd
   read the funny papers
with *"Happy Jack."*
Those were the days
   when stars were stars
   and in their proper place.
Those were the days
   when clouds were clouds

and a rock was a rock
and the sun stayed up
all day 'til night
and, *"Time to go to bed,*
there's school tomorrow!"
"Good" old days,
not like these,
good *"old"* days.

HAPPY BIRTHDAY

4/80

Happy birthday, foot!
Walked on any water, lately?

Happy birthday, arm!
Waved any goodbyes, today?
Any hellos?

Happy birthday, brains!
Had any good thoughts
upon which to occupy yourself?

This is the 19,176th
day of our life.
What a glorious day
to be alive, folks!
One of the best I've ever had.
I still see pretty well
and hear very well
and the rest of my senses
haven't suffered much
for being almost

20,000 days old.

Happy birthday, self!
You've done a good job
just living this long.

I sure am proud of you
    and wish you
    19,000 more
beautiful days of life,
    even better
than the last 19,000.
    Happy birthday, me!

THE JUMPER

4/80

The man in the red suit
    leaps
from the high plane,
    opens
his artificial red wings
    and plummets,
    head down,
in tight circles
    toward earth.

At the critical moment
    falls back,
releasing his wings
    that float back,
    up, off
and out of sight.

With precise
    gymnastic form
executes
    a perfect,
    mid-air
front jump.

The man
    in the red suit,
falling free,
    feet first,
    toes pointed,
    knees of steel,
    hands to sides,
    spine erect,
    shoulders down,
    head and neck aligned,
confident
    at 2,000 feet,
hurtling,
    feet first,
toward the bay
    and cold water.

He approaches the water,
    and with perfect timing,
jackknifes,
    head first,
    into the cold bay.
He does not sink,
    but pops up fast.

Later, in the outboard,
    we pick him up.

A tanned oriental face,
   strong jaw,
   clear eyes,
   intelligent.
His head and torso
   like an ancient ivory sculpture.
His shoulders thick and wide,
   his chest slim and strong.
I think I detect
   a long scar
at the side of his ribs,
   then, startled,
I see
   his upper arms
   are merged with
   and have grown
to the sides of his chest.

We return through the lobby,
   the jumper, shirtless,
in tie-up pants
   and thongs.
I find, recently,
   it is of general knowledge
he is a champion boxer
   as well.

Notes - Acceptance

The emotional processing of 1979 gradually became self-acceptance in 1980. I had reached a new level of self awareness, the immensely difficult decision to leave my marriage had been made, life with my new friend was becoming more familiar, my general direction regarding work and offspring was clearer, and what remained was hard work in doing the tasks before me. As in my first poetic attempt in 1966, *A Clear Picture,* my window, *ever dirtier,* had *caused the pain to make me clean* and pain was finally *bearable once again.* Other pains were to be faced, of course; financial difficulties in supporting two households, selling our home in a down market *(a condition of the divorce),* and continuing uncertainties involving our teenage daughters. The tough questions; *"Who am I?, What am I doing here?, Why doesn't life reality match life dream?",* were essentially answered. It was crucial I act in light of the new information according to new circumstances, and during the year I put my energy to that effort.

Winter Rains accepts that sweet and bitter things are inseparable and sometimes it's gratifying to love the bitter. *From the Teeming Center of the Agitated Mind,* for me, is an expression of *'is-ness,'* that is, there is no right or wrong, proper or improper, there is only what is, a comforting Zen-like insight I gladly accepted in 1980. I have things yet to understand in *Voice in the Mist,* but promised I will. No longer alone because I have *'self'* for company, I don't fear destiny in *Content, Free, Falling.* In *Your Natural Right,* I continue to claim space. *The Crow,* symbol of pervasive negative judgment, remains, but has lost its power.

It is curious my first poetic attempt in 1966, *A Clear Picture,* pointed ten years into the future to the onset of my marital and family crisis in 1976. How could I have known so many years in advance what my major life task would be; to pass from living an unaware life to pursuing an aware one? Who inside me knew I had buried *'self'* or *'feelings'* and decided on doing *'poetic-ness'* as a way of recovery? The little fish in *Blue the Grass of the Happier Heart* of course.

To be a good poet, you can't be afraid to write a bad poem. This comforting philosophy permitted me to risk poetry writing that led me to *Roethke* writing to automatic writing and dream analysis. The combination allowed me to uncover ancient, long-obsolete survival patterns which were not so subtly impinging on present life, and discard them. Unwanted defenses gone, what remained was my formerly repressed essential self, *The Heartsore.* In the past ten years I have let him dry out, get some exercise, become used to being unfettered and encouraged him to live, love and adventure without the inhibiting constraints of an antiquated defensive system.

Since 1980, I've learned my traumatic near-death experience at 17 months and subsequent unnatural son-mother bond was exacerbated by a family dynamic in which I played the role of artistic, intellectual partner for mother; one which my father, having little formal education or other cultural interest, could not play. Already bonded by an early traumatic experience, I ignorantly assumed the role of *'half-mate'* to mother in artistic and intellectual matters, without the other usual marital privileges. When I first married,

I chose someone to whom I could not be close so as not to betray former *'half-wife,'* mother. I lived what I call a *'parallel life'* to the one I'd have lived, had I not been traumatically or chronically warped.

I often wonder what my shadow life, my life without neurosis, might have been following the pure dictates of my trusting, congruent *'self.'* Would life's dreams have matched life's reality? If hypertension hadn't kept me from armed service, would I have fought and died in Korea? Would I have chosen architecture as a career? Would I have married a different woman for life? Would I have had three beautiful, unique and self-actuating daughters and a miraculous second wife who has brought three additional daughters and a son into our family, whom I love and who love me? Would . . . ? Would . . . ? Would . . . ?

As my new friend says, *"The most feared powers, once found and understood, become energy."* The severest pains, overcome, are frequently the source of our greatest strengths. I believe everything that happens in the world is correct and I wouldn't trade what happened in my life because the unique things that happened to me are what make my life *mine. The Jumper* has an exhilarating adventure. Leaping from the high plane, he circles and his artificial wings come off. He descends feet first, body aligned, and with perfect timing, executes a perfect move. We notice he is scarred - by what previous injury? Clearly, something dire happened. We see he is healthy, capable and can do many things. I, of course, am *The Jumper.* I know because I dreamed him.

ONE SPIRIT

4/80

The crescent moon
came stealing across the country highway.
Its quiet light
permeated the cornfields and cornstalks
and sifted its chalky powder
    deep into the wheat fields
rising in the summer night.
    The pavement shone
like thousands of moonstones
    laid in a silvery ribbon
lacing the black hills.
    Venus lifted her head
just above the mountainous silhouette
    and other stars
assumed their places
    in the blue-black heavens.
It was time for me
    to meld myself
    into my essence
and assume one spirit,
    indivisible.

INDEX OF PERSONAL SYMBOLS

The meaning of these symbols became clear as I worked on the dream interpretations automatic poems.

Emanuel	Joyful spirit.
Fish	Survival self.
Crow	Punitive parent or *"conscience."*
Beetle	Active self. *(As against <u>re</u>-active self.)*
Dove	Benevolent deity.
Stone	Rightful and eternal being.
April	False promise of delight.
Rain	Blissful peace.
Elephants	Traumatic child experience.
Heartsore	Repressed self about to be accepted.
Nature	Balance to feelings of despair.
Charred trunks	Personage in world unconnected with self.
Dolly	Delightfully accepted self.
Oranges	Capacity for love/passion discovered later in life.
Yellow roses or lemons	Loving father spirit.
Trees	Life's promise fulfilled.

OTHER BOOKS BY DOUG RUCKER

TRIAL BY FIRE - A Tale of Two Houses
Autobiography and Architecture

EARLY STORIES
Autobiography years 1927 thru 1950

GROUNDWORK
Autobiography years 1950 thru 1964

MOVING THROUGH
Poetry, 400 pages, years 1966 thru 1984

GROWING EDGE
Autobiography years 1964 thru 1970

BOOK OF WORDS
Sixty-seven homey essays

WHERE'S THE COOKIES AT?
Seventy-seven nonsensical essays

HAROLD AND THE ACID SEA OF REALITY
Sixty-eight essays on life

REFLECTIONS
Art - 25 color reflection photos with text

OFF THE WALL
Art - 25 digitally manipulated photos of graffiti

ACKNOWLEDGEMENTS

I wish to thank Marge Lewi-Rucker, my caring wife, who gave unceasingly of her love, knowledge and spirit and without whom my personal process would have taken years longer. I want to express gratitude to Helane Freeman without whose knowledge of InDesign, the computer and publishing experience this book would have been impossible. Appreciatin goes to my lovely daughters, Viveka, Lilianne, and Amanda. Their personal lives helped point my way to a more healthful existence; gratitude goes to Marge's children, Jennifer, Katy, Christopher and Marggy, and my father and mother, Philip and Evelyn Rucker whom I've always loved and who've given me their best; and to brother, David, who, despite my falsely superior attitude during our adolescence, loves me still. I wish to appreciate my close personal friend, Rick Davidson *(1933-1999)*, architect, poet, writer, who lent me the courage to enter the poetic adventure and whose loving spirit bolstered me during the most difficult times. Susan Pollock, Dance Therapist, now deceased, will forever occupy a warm place in my heart as will dance group members, Marge, Susan, Dirk, Claire, Skylar, Margaret, Dottie, Barbara, Ron, Andrea, and Tres, lovingly led by *'the teach'* Debra Feltman. MFCC Intern, Susan Schreyer, must be credited for accepting me in her psychological program. I'd like to express my appreciation to Ron Munro, my personal friend and client, who introduced me to the computer and word processing and to diseased Jack Birdsall who worked diligently with me for years getting this and other works published in book form. Also, I wish to tell all who understood my situation, I felt your caring and compassion and it helped me more than I can express.

A BRIEF BIOGRAPHY

*A*fter a grammer school scholarship to the Chicago Art Institute, Doug entered Austin High School where he lettered in football, track and swimming while pursuing a three-year course in architecture. At the University of Illinois in Champaign-Urbana with a steady meal job, he graduated with an architectural Bachelor of Science degree in architecture. After graduation he worked as draftsman in Denver and San Diego. In Pasadena, he married his first wife, Karon Conan, and received his California State architectural license. In a house of his own design in Santa Monica Canyon, Karon gave birth to three daughters. During his 54 year career in his own office in Malibu, in 1966, he built their own Malibu *'dream house,'* the main floor floating on a 26-foot-square pedestal, 35 feet in the air, with a wraparound deck and spectacular views of the estuary and Surfrider Beach. After numerous publications, it was burned to the ground late in 1970. By 1972, he'd built another more fire resistant and equally-dramatic house over the same foundations It was similarly honored and published, but lost to a divorce in 1980. Doug and Marjory, his new wife of 25 years, are enjoying a creative life in a very small house with two separate studios on an acre of land in the mountains above and between Agoura Hills and Malibu. Semi-retired, he's enjoying writing books and showing his reflective and abstract photography in the area's numerous art galleries.

www.ingramcontent.com/pod-product-compliance
Lightning Source LLC
Chambersburg PA
CBHW071954260326
41914CB00004B/799